The Historic Hotels of London

A Select Guide

WENDY ARNOLD

The Historic Hotels of London

A Select Guide

Photographs by
ROBIN MORRISON

Revised edition

THAMES AND HUDSON

For Ian and Nikki, Robin and Kim, and Tiffany

Frontispiece: a doorman in splendid livery stands on the steps of the Arlington Street entrance to The Ritz, ready to greet visitors. See p. 77.

Opposite: the Chinese Room in Blakes is typical of this hotel's richly decorated sophisticated interiors. See p. 19.

First published in Great Britain in 1986
Revised edition published 1989

© 1986, 1989 Thames and Hudson Ltd, London

Typeset in Monophoto Plantin Light

Printed and bound in Hong Kong

Contents

Preface

Tower Bridge and the Thames, seen through a window in 'Captain Webb', a Victorian barge converted into a luxury hotel. See p. 29.

See p. 29.

I never tire of London. Few great cities are so full of flowers and tree-filled squares: parks that were once the hunting grounds of Elizabeth I stretch from the gates of Buckingham Palace to the statue of Peter Pan in Kensington Gardens, in one almost unbroken vista. St Paul's Cathedral still crowns the City, rising above Roman walls and the Norman Tower, Georgian pillars, and Victorian chimneys, shaming the architects of the modern blank-faced office blocks. In the Mall, cavalry magnificent in plumed helmets and shining breastplates trot past to change the guard; you may suddenly glimpse the Queen's face in the depths of the vast limousine gliding by. The Houses of Parliament are now a golden Gothic fantasy: like many of London's finest buildings they have recently been rescued from their coating of urban grime. Theater and opera, exhibitions and galleries, antique shops and gourmet restaurants offer a bewildering choice. The question is, where to stay while sampling all these delights?

London has a great wealth of historic hotels, many also restored in recent years to glittering splendor. At the cost of millions, they have regained their turn-of-the-century magnificence. Doormen in cockaded top hats usher guests out of their taxis, tea is served in silver on a starched cloth, fresh flowers are everywhere in great cascading displays, and the 20th century intrudes only to ensure the comforts of central heating and modern plumbing.

Three years ago I first explored and wrote about London's hotels. Since then I have spent most of my time visiting and writing about historic hotels in Scotland, France, and Ireland. In between trips I have stayed in London hotels to keep an eye on those I had selected, and to be sure they were maintaining standards. I sampled any new chef's menus, appeared unannounced and unnoticed at busy times to see how staff were coping, and advised demanding friends where to stay, asking them to report back. I have also stayed in new or newly refurbished hotels. As always, I do not accept any hospitality, free meals, or fees for inclusion in this book. To my original choice I have added only those I found to be welcoming, comfortable, and spotlessly clean. All have charming decor and friendly staff, and offer what I consider to be good value for the prices charged.

One recent development is that an increasing number of owners of historic country hotels are opening often delightful small London establishments. Most have chosen to recreate the blend of chintz, antiques, open fires, fresh flowers, and attentive staff that have made country house hotels so popular, and so much appreciated by guests who do not seek palatial public rooms, boutiques, or many-course meals. Most, given excellent eating places nearby, have no restaurant, but serve civilized snacks. Staying in them is rather like visiting unobtrusive but cherishing friends who own a particularly fine London house.

Majestic or modest, these are the hotels I believe you will most enjoy when visiting London.

General Information

Preparation It is always wise to book as far in advance as possible, to avoid disappointment. June through September are especially busy months. The map at the end of the book, and notes at the end of each entry, show the location of the hotel, and give an indication of nearby parking, shopping, and sight-seeing. The charm of historic hotels is that rooms are not standardized, so make a specific request when booking if you want a spacious room, plenty of closet space, a shower, a 6-foot bed, antique or modern furnishing, a quiet situation at the back away from traffic, or do not want to climb a lot of stairs. Bring layers of clothing, at least one warm outfit, and a light raincoat even in summer, as you may meet heatwave, cold snap, or downpour. Dress for theater or opera as you please, from jeans to tiaras, but note that most restaurants request ties.

Terms Prices and exchange rates fluctuate, so I have divided hotels into three general categories, based on their charge for two people sharing a standard room for one night and having a continental breakfast. I have included the obligatory tax VAT (currently 15%) and a service charge of 10%. When you enquire about prices, note that many hotels quote VAT and service separately. Please note that I have not included telephone calls, drinks, or other extras such as full English breakfast, except when they are included in the cost of a room. Enquire about special seasonal or bargain breaks. (The dollar equivalent is based on a rate of exchange of £1 = $1.70.)

Accommodation for two people sharing for one night
Moderate   £ 55–115 (approx. $ 94–196)
Expensive   £120–175 (approx. $204–298)
Deluxe   £190–225 (approx. $323–383)

The cost of meals other than breakfast is quoted separately:

Meals for two
Moderate   £24–33 (approx. $41–56)
Expensive   £34–49 (approx. $58–83)
Deluxe   £50–110 (approx $85–188)

This represents the average price of an *à la carte* meal without wine, but including tax, service at 10% and any cover charge. Many hotels offer a fixed-price *table-d'hôte* menu, and I have mentioned if this is available. Special low price pre-theater dinners may be offered; some hotels have no restaurant but offer light snacks.

Hotels which are not hotels I have included some interesting alternatives to staying in an actual hotel, including a boat, a small house to hire by the week, and a private home. Read details carefully, as conditions of stay vary. To make bookings for private house holidays contact: In The English Manner, Lancych, Boncath, Pembrokeshire, Wales SA37 0LJ (tel: 0239 77378), or Wolsey Lodges, 17 Chapel Street, Bildeston, Suffolk IP7 7EP (tel. 0449 740609).

Transport Parking is difficult in London. I have noted where it is provided by hotels; if it is not, I have indicated where it is available close by. This is usually in a fee-paying National Car Park (NCP). The drivers of London's traditional taxi cabs undergo extensive training lasting up to 2 years, are given detailed examinations of their local knowledge, are checked by doctors and police before receiving licences, and must by law maintain their vehicles both inside and out. Minicab drivers are usually unlicensed and unchecked. Underground (tube) trains are often a fast way to get around, but can spring nasty surprises such as out-of-action moving stairs and lengthy passageways linking different lines. Red London buses give excellent views of the city from their top deck, but move slowly in rush hours. Concessionary passes for varying periods on tube and bus offer a bargain to dedicated sightseers (they are sometimes available abroad: enquire at English tourist offices).

Sightseeing *What's On* and *Time Out* are weekly magazines giving information on theaters, cinemas, restaurants, etc. *Historic Houses, Castles and Gardens in Great Britain and Ireland*, published annually in the UK, gives opening times and admission charges. London street maps are useful, especially *Inner London in Super Scale*, published by the Geographers' A–Z Map Co. *Eating Out in London* and *Shopping in London*, published by *Time Out* magazine, are very detailed and modestly priced annual guides to London's restaurants and shops. All are readily available at bookstalls.

Footnote This is a personal selection of hotels and other establishments that proved delightful to stay in, to which I would happily return, and where with confidence I would send even my most exacting friends. Should a problem arise, tell the owners or managers. It helps them to know, though it would gladden their day also to hear of anything you particularly enjoyed about your stay. I too should be most grateful to hear any comments, care of the publishers.

A gracious mansion

The Abbey Court, a handsome Victorian mansion, is one of the delightful little hotels now appearing in London that have been created by country-house hotel owners. They emulate the former tradition of the English gentry, who used to maintain both a large mansion in the country and an elegant establishment in town. Nicholas Crawley was in fact associated with two country-house hotels, Middlethorpe Hall near York, dating from 1700 (see my *Historic Country Hotels of England*), and a medieval manor, Bodysgallen Hall in Wales, both much-acclaimed.

Entirely furnished in antiques, trophies of a patient and lengthy hunt through the Yorkshire Dales, The Abbey Court has been rescued from its slide into shabby decay, and become once again a gracious mansion. The whole street has been gentrified, painted, and restored, since it is in an area rich in fashionable little restaurants and conveniently close to the antique dealers' happy hunting grounds of the Portobello Road and Kensington Church Street. A new stone balustrade encloses a tiny forecourt spilling over with flower-filled tubs. Steps lead to the front door, gleaming with well-polished brass, and into a high-ceilinged, pleasantly uncluttered hall with a charming flower-arrangement. There is a comfortable small sitting room furnished in chintz beside the reception desk. My bedroom on the ground floor at the back lacked a view but was very peaceful. The superb four-poster was lined with cream-colored pleated glazed cotton with a pattern of tiny brown leaves and the same fabric also edged the chintz bedspread and covered the easy chairs. The fitted carpet was pale green, the dressing table and round bedside tables draped in a darker green; there were crinkled-glass-bottle lamps, and an antique gilded mirror. On the walls were framed panels of Chinese embroidery, foxhunting and botanical prints. The bathroom, tiled in a gray Italian marble, had an enormous and marvellously inundating shower-head, as well as a whirlpool tub, brass taps, and plenty of toiletries. I arrived before the chef was installed. A former purveyor of director's private luncheons, she should by now be ensuring a 24-hour room-service of delectable light meals. However, when I declared hunger, I was enterprisingly fed some most acceptable ham sandwiches, freshly baked cookies, fresh fruit, and coffee. They were set – as was my next day's excellent breakfast – with correct formality on shining silverware and pretty Villeroy and Boch flower-pattern china, set on a starched white cloth.

Former guests of Mr Crawley's country retreats seeking a quiet and attractively decorated hotel not far from Holland Park will find The Abbey Court a perfect London base.

The pillared portico of this elegant town house (opposite) leads to comfortable rooms, entirely furnished with antiques. One of the luxurious bathrooms is shown above.

THE ABBEY COURT, 20 Pembridge Gardens, W2 4DU. **Map reference** 2. **Tel.** (01) 221 7518. **Telex** 262 167 AbbyCt. **Fax** (01) 792 0858. **Owners** City and Capital Hotels. **Manager** Graham Chapman. **Open** All year. **Rooms** 17 double (inc. 3 four-posters), 5 single, all with bathroom (with showers and whirlpool tubs), direct-dial phone, TV. **Facilities** Small sitting room, 24-hr room service. NB No elevator. **Restrictions** No children under 12. **Terms** Moderate. Ask about special breaks. **Lunch/Dinner** Moderate (snacks only). **Credit cards** All major cards. **Nearest tube station** Notting Hill Gate, 50 yds (Queensway and Bayswater nearby also). **Hotel parking** Sometimes in street. Nearest NCP in Queensway. **Local eating** Clarke's, 124 Kensington Church Street, W8; Geales, 2 Farmer Street, W8; Julie's, 135 Portland Road, W11; One Nine Two, 192 Kensington Park Road, W11; Hiroko of Kensington, Kensington Hilton, 179 Holland Park Avenue, W11. **Local shopping** Portobello market; Kensington Church Street antique shops; Kensington High Street. **Local interest** Portobello market; Holland Park; Kensington Gardens; London Toy and Model Museum. NB This part of London varies from the very chic to the rough; ask the hotel to identify the most pleasant areas.

Edwardian seclusion

Mayfair, now London's most fashionable district, was until the end of the 18th century a thoroughly disreputable area of open fields. A fair was held there under charter from James II, "on the first day of May, to continue for fourteen days after, yearly, for ever." To see mountebanks and jugglers, conjurers and puppet shows, fire-eaters and prize-fighters, tigers and elephants, tightrope walkers and ladies of ill repute, a great noisy drunken crowd gathered there. Pockets were picked, fortunes were lost on the gaming table, and illegal marriages were performed in a chapel by a reprobate clergyman at any hour of the day or night, no questions asked. With the building of Berkeley and Grosvenor Squares, and of stately mansions along Piccadilly and Park Lane, the fields began to disappear and the nobility started to complain about the noise and disorderly conduct of the riff-raff. In 1809 the May Fair was finally suppressed, leaving only its name, but Shepherd Market, where the crowds made their purchases, still remains, a fascinating jumble of narrow streets and ancient buildings.

Just a step away, in a row of neat, turn-of-the-century houses with bay windows, iron railings, and colorful windowboxes, are the Athenaeum Apartments. Immaculately maintained, luxuriously comfortable, they are an alternative to a hotel suite and provide the added advantages of privacy and a fully equipped modern all-electric kitchen. A jogging map is provided for the athletic, since Green Park is just the other side of Piccadilly, and tracksuits are available on request. Buckingham Palace, the lake and gardens of St James's Park, and many of London's most elegant shops and restaurants are close by.

My apartment had its own hallway, impeccable pine kitchen, and gleaming modern bathroom. The bedroom, furnished in toning shades of rust and beige, was equipped with a six-feet-wide double bed, prettily draped with curtains in a delicate leaf pattern, a deep walk-in clothes closet, color television, direct-dial phone, and a comfortable velvet armchair. The spacious living room had fabrics with an antique pattern of birds and plants, dining table and chairs, and a further phone and television.

The apartments belong to, and are at the back of, the excellent and attentive Athenaeum Hotel on Piccadilly, which provides everything offered to its own guests except room service and will stock refrigerators in the apartments on request. It has a panelled bar specializing in Scottish malt whiskies, a charming restaurant, and delicious afternoon teas, all adding to the enjoyment of a stay in this exclusive home from home.

Opposite: top, an elegant sitting room in one of the apartments; bottom, the dining room in the adjoining Athenaeum Hotel. Above: a king-sized bed in an apartment bedroom.

ATHENAEUM APARTMENTS, Down Street, W1V 0BJ. For booking, contact Athenaeum Hotel, 116 Piccadilly, W1V 0BJ. **Map reference** 14. **Tel.** Athenaeum Hotel: (01) 499 3464. **Telex** 261589 ATHOME. **Fax** (01) 493 1860. **Owners** Rank Hotels. **Manager** Nicholas Rettie. **Open** All year. **Rooms** 40 double-bedroom apartments, 3 two-bedroom apartments, all with bathroom (including shower), kitchen, color TV, 2 or 3 direct-dial or operator phones, radio. **Facilities** Entry phone, elevator, porter service, Mon.–Fri. maid service, same-day laundry/dry-cleaning/valeting service (weekdays only), baby sitting. In hotel: bar, lounge, restaurant, 3 private reception suites, beauty salon, in-house nurse, hospitality service to meet/greet and advise first-time vistors, photocopying and document delivery service, safe. **Restrictions** No dogs (guidedogs excepted). **Terms** Moderate. **Lunch** (in hotel) Expensive. Moderate fixed-price menu. **Dinner** Deluxe. Moderate fixed-price menu and moderate fixed-price pre-theater suppers. **Credit cards** All major cards. **Nearest tube station** Green Park, ¼ mile. **Hotel parking** Yes, but limited. **Local eating** Mirabelle, 56 Curzon Street, W1; The Greenhouse, 27a Hay's Mews, W1; The Ritz (see p. 77). **Local shopping** Bond Street; Burlington Arcade; Fortnum and Mason's and other Piccadilly stores; Cork Street commercial art galleries. **Local interest** Green Park; Buckingham Palace; Apsley House (Duke of Wellington museum) and Hyde Park; Royal Academy; Museum of Mankind.

Old-world charm

The impressive room to the left of the entrance in the Basil Street Hotel started life as a booking hall for the underground railway. By the time the Taylor family bought the hotel in 1919, this had become an elegant ballroom, much in demand in an era when the landed gentry came to London to have their daughters presented at Court, and stayed on for the London season of parties and balls. Today it is a club, set aside for lady guests of the hotel and country members coming up for the day to shop at Harrods, which is just at the other end of Basil Street.

Narrow marble steps lead to a half gallery, where you sign in. A friendly reception girl will take you up in the one tiny elevator to long, light corridors, off which are the comfortable and surprisingly quiet bedrooms, all with fine bedlinen. The pine-panelled or tiled bathrooms have excellent showers, and many are very large, since they were originally single bedrooms.

The hotel has a gracious Edwardian entrance hall, with an oriental carpet, potted palms, fresh flowers, and a graceful staircase leading up to a large lounge, where comfortable, chintz-covered easy chairs in well-spaced groups create a club-like atmosphere. A bell on the wall can be rung to summon a waiter to bring morning coffee, afternoon tea, or drinks. A long gallery, with windowed alcoves on one side, each with a writing desk, has large antique vases, paintings on glass, polished woodblock floors, and dark red and blue carpets. It leads to a stately panelled restaurant, painted pale green and candlelit at night, which serves traditional English food. A coffee shop upstairs offers buffet meals, snacks, and sandwiches to guests, shoppers, and local office-workers; downstairs is a cellar wine-bar for those not wanting a formal restaurant meal.

People enjoy The Basil. An American Ladies' Club was happily lunching there at a long table beside mine, and I was nearly swamped on the stairs by an eager rush of small girls dressed as clowns and clutching elegantly wrapped gifts, coming to a party. In the words of Stephen Korany, General Manager for more than 35 years, there is something special about a place that has been in the same family for 80 years. Although not the most grandiose hotel in London, The Basil is certainly one of the best loved.

Opposite: the main staircase, which leads up to the Lounge.
Above: an inviting easy chair in a corner of this comfortable hotel.

THE BASIL STREET HOTEL, Basil Street, SW3 1AH. **Map reference** 12. **Tel.** (01) 581 3311. **Telex** 28379 **Fax** (01) 581 3693. **Owner** Private partnership. **General Manager** Stephen Korany. **Open** All year. **Rooms** 48 single, 44 double, 1 suite, 71 with bathroom (with shower over tub) and hairdryer, all with color TV, direct-dial phone, and radio. **Facilities** 24-hr. room service, elevator, 24-hr. laundry/drycleaning/valeting service (weekdays only), ladies' club room, lounge, restaurant, writing rooms, private reception and conference rooms, safe. **Restrictions** No dogs in public rooms. **Terms** Moderate. **Lunch/Dinner** (in restaurant) Moderate. Only fixed-price menu at lunchtime. **Credit cards** All major cards. **Nearest tube station** Knightsbridge, 150 yds. **Hotel parking** No. NCP off Basil Street, 100 yds. **Local eating** The Capital and Le Metro, Basil Street, SW3 (see pp. 27 and 55); Harrod's snackbars; GTC, Sloane Street, SW1, for light meals. **Local shopping** Harrods, Harvey Nichols, Scotch House, and other Knightsbridge stores; Peter Jones; King's Road and Sloane Street boutiques. **Local interest** Royal Albert Hall; Hyde Park and Kensington Gardens for jogging, riding, and boating; Natural History, Science, Geological, and Victoria & Albert museums.

14

Formal comforts

Apsley House, on Hyde Park Corner, has the impressive address "Number One, London." It is still the town house of the Dukes of Wellington and the first duke's soldiers, who fought at the Battle of Waterloo, used to drill on a barracks square opposite, where The Berkeley now stands.

The hotel's owners, the Savoy group, boldly moved name, traditions, silver, linen, fireplaces, wood panelling, antique clocks, pictures, and a complete room by famous architect Sir Edwin Lutyens from the original Mayfair site to an entirely new airconditioned, double-glazed, centrally-heated building with a penthouse swimming pool and subterranean garage. Corridor carpets were specially woven from a 13th-century embroidery design discovered in a French cathedral and Michael Inchbold and other top designers were called in to create elegant private reception rooms and suites. Nobody knew whether the clientèle of the old hotel, whose loyalty had been built up over a hundred years, would approve. They did.

There is nothing of the brash modern hotel about this new Berkeley. Uniformed doormen greet you politely, porters efficiently whisk your luggage away, and elegantly clothed, very correct young managers formally dressed in black jackets first conduct you to an antique desk to sign in, then escort you to your room or suite, to make certain that it is to your satisfaction. The bedrooms, each of which has its own anteroom, are not standardized in any way. Some are traditional, with dark wood panelling, velvet upholstery, antique furniture, and chandeliers, others are modern, with light chintzes and prints. All have modern bathrooms ranging from the large to the enormous.

Rooms on the top floor have little balconies overlooking London, and are near the elegant penthouse swimming pool, which has its own restaurant, a flower-bedecked sunning area, a gymnasium, sauna, and a sliding roof for inclement weather. For dinner there is a choice between the main restaurant and the elegant Buttery, where I enjoyed a delicious meal. The selection of *hors d'oeuvres* was outstanding, and rack of lamb with fresh vegetables, followed by mango icecream, were superb. There is an encyclopedic wine list, compiled with great expertise. After a luxuriously comfortable night, Sunday morning brought a brief but penetrating peal of bells from St Paul's church next door, and an excellent breakfast, served on pretty blue-green Wedgwood china. The Berkeley is a hotel which is at the same time traditionally historic and conveniently modern. A remarkable achievement.

Opposite: in the restaurant diners can enjoy the trompe l'oeil view of Apsley House while sampling a delicious dessert from the trolley. A typically appealing bedroom is shown above; overleaf is the magnificent penthouse pool, which has a roof that is slid open in fine weather.

THE BERKELEY, Wilton Place, SW1X 7RL. **Map reference** 9. **Tel.** (01) 235 6000. **Telex** 919252. **Owners** The Savoy Hotel plc. **General Manager** Stefano Sebastiani. **Open** All year. **Rooms** 133 rooms, 27 suites (3 with conservatories), all with bathroom (including shower), foyers, airconditioning, doubleglazing, color TV, radio. **Facilities** 24-hr. room service, maid, valet, and waiter service, 2-day or express same-day drycleaning/laundry/valeting services, elevators, restaurant and Buttery, bar, Lutyens Room, ballroom, reception rooms, swimming pool, saunas, massage, beauty treatments, barber, beauty shop, gymnasium, baby-sitting, safe, cinema, flower shop, garage; special all-inclusive, fixed-exchange rate, seasonal breaks; picnic hampers for sporting outings by arrangement. **Restrictions** No dogs. **Terms** Deluxe. **Lunch/Dinner** (in both restaurant and Buttery) Deluxe. **Credit cards** All major cards. **Nearest tube station** Hyde Park Corner, 100 yds. **Hotel parking** Yes (capacity 50 cars). **Local eating** The Capital Hotel and Le Metro, Basil Street, SW3 (see pp. 27 and 55), The Greenhouse, 27a Hay's Mews, W1. **Local shopping** Harrods and other Knightsbridge stores; Sloane Street and King's Road boutiques. **Local interest** Hyde Park; Buckingham Palace and St James's Palace; Royal Albert Hall; Natural History, Science, Geological, and Victoria & Albert museums; Duke of Wellington Museum in Apsley House.

Blakes

Fashionable flair

Blakes shows just what exciting things can be done to a row of fairly ordinary 19th-century houses. A new foyer has been added, but the rest of the hotel is a fascinating blend of modern and Victorian. In the reception area, a vast square umbrella stands over the stairs leading down to the restaurant. A mountain of the sort of luggage that accompanied a 19th-century explorer stands as though waiting for Stanley's bearers to lift it to their shoulders and set off in search of Livingstone. It is topped by a cage containing a pretty pink and green parakeet that I thought was stuffed, until it startled me by moving. There is a background color scheme of black and white lightened by dove-gray and refreshing moss green. The reception girls are cool, elegant, and extremely efficient, the porter cheerful and friendly.

This fashionable haunt of media people has the faintly world-weary air of those accustomed to the presence of the famous and the wealthy. Guests frequently arrive at strange hours of the night, having flown in from California, or having just finished a lengthy recording session. Whatever meal is currently offered in the restaurant can also be served in the rooms, supported by a most comprehensive 24-hour room-service menu. The selection is tailored to the tastes of a sophisticated international clientèle and offers bortsch, blini, sashimi, satay, szechwan duck, and coffee with cardamon, as well as roast lamb, fudge cake, bacon-lettuce-and-tomato toasted sandwiches, live yoghurt with banana, wheat germ, and clover honey. The mirror-lined restaurant is modern, with round tables covered with black or white cloths alternately. Low square glass vases stuffed with bright lilies add splashes of color.

Pre-dinner drinks and after-dinner coffee are served in the Chinese Room, where soft squishy chairs line the walls round a vast square table piled high with art books and magazines. Talk tends to be of contracts and festivals, success at Cannes, or returning to location in Tunisia. With difficulty I stopped myself greeting as an old friend somebody whose face was familiar to me only because it appeared daily on my television screen.

The stylish bedrooms, reached by an elevator, are all different. Some have four-posters, sumptuously decked in heavy wild silk. Mine had vast mirrors, white paintwork, green and white lattice-patterned drapes and bedcover, a large potted palm, and a gleamingly clean gray and white bathroom with big white towels. Storage space was ample. This is a sophisticated, laid-back, and efficiently run hotel of great personality.

Opposite: two glimpses of the stylish bedrooms; the model of Marlene Dietrich (above) is on the bar. The glamorous interiors overleaf are, left, a bathroom and, right, the Chinese Room, where guests relax after dinner.

BLAKES, 33 Roland Gardens, SW7 3PF. **Map reference** 3. **Tel.** (01) 370 6701. **Telex** 8813500. **Fax** (01) 373 0442. **Owner** Anouska Hempel Weinberg. **Manager** Robert Wauters. **Open** All year. **Rooms** 13 single, 24 double, 12 suites/mini-apartments, all with bathroom (including shower), color TV, direct-dial phone, mini-bar, safe. **Facilities** Elevator, restaurant, Chinese Room, bar, 24-hr. room service, safe, same-day laundry/dry cleaning/valeting (weekdays only), conservatory. Health club nearby. **Restrictions** None. **Terms** Expensive. **Lunch/Dinner** Deluxe. **Credit cards** All major cards. **Nearest tube station** South Kensington, ½ mile. **Hotel parking** No.

Nearest is at Gloucester Hotel, 4 Harrington Gardens, SW7. **Local eating** Blue Elephant, 4–5 Fulham Broadway, SW6; Hilaire, 68 Old Brompton Rd, SW7; Bibendum, Michelin Building, 81 Fulham Rd, SW3; L'Arlequin, 123 Queenstown Road, SW8 (across the Thames: my favorite London restaurant). **Local shopping** King's Road and Fulham Road boutiques; Anouska Hempel Couture, 2 Pond Place, SW3; Harrods and Knightsbridge stores (1 mile). **Local interest** Kensington Gardens and Palace; Royal Albert Hall; South Kensington museums.

Traditional excellence

When vising Brown's Hotel, Queen Victoria used to sit in the blue velvet chair with glided legs and arms that is proudly preserved, together with an identical second chair (for Prince Albert, perhaps?), in a curtained alcove at the top of the stairs. In front of them is a fine ornate antique desk, at which author Rudyard Kipling worked when staying here. Over the years many crowned heads and world leaders have selected Brown's rather than one of London's more imposing establishments, perhaps because, being made up of fourteen small Georgian and Victorian houses, it feels much more like a private residence than a hotel. The reception rooms are low ceilinged and wood panelled, with alcoves and antiques, fat velvet chairs, and plenty of fresh flowers. Each bedroom has an individual character, with pretty wallpaper, toning bedcovers and paintwork, ample clothes space, a good bathroom, mini-bar, and color television: some have airconditioning.

Although bought several years ago by Trusthouse Forte, Brown's has wisely been allowed to keep its own traditions of attentive personal service, established in 1837 by James Brown, a retired gentleman's gentleman, in one little house in Dover Street. With the assistance of his wife, a former lady's maid to Lord Byron's widow, he built up a reputation for such excellent service that another four adjoining houses were purchased, catering admirably to the influx of visitors that came to the Great Exhibition of 1851 in nearby Hyde Park. His successor introduced all sorts of modern marvels to the hotel: electricity, fixed baths with piped water, and telephones – Alexander Graham Bell made one of Britain's first phone calls from Brown's. Theodore Roosevelt was married from the hotel, and his cousin Franklin stayed here for part of his honeymoon.

When I first knew Brown's, it was a quiet, traditional, slightly faded place where nicely-brought-up girls from the country might stay respectably, and where fires were still lit for guests in the bedroom grates. Now it is elegant and impeccable, and many of the voices overheard at the fashionable afternoon teatime are transatlantic, exclaiming with pleasure over the pink wild-rose-patterned Wedgwood china, and the well-provisioned three-tiered cake stands. Champagne teas are a new fashion. Dinner in the delightful panelled restaurant attracts an even more international clientèle. The selection of wines is perfectly balanced, from the unassuming to the outstanding, and is sensibly priced. I think that James Brown would be pleased to see how, after a century and a half, the highest standards are still maintained in his hotel.

Brown's is famous for its afternoon teas (opposite); one of its attractive and very comfortable bedrooms is shown above.

BROWN'S HOTEL, Albemarle and Dover Streets, W1A 4SW. **Map reference** 22. **Tel.** (01) 493 6020. **Telex** 28686. **Fax** (01) 493 9381. **Owners** Trusthouse Forte. **General Manager** Bruce Banister. **Open** All year. **Rooms** 19 single, 89 double, 25 suites, all with bathroom (including shower), color TV, mini-bar, direct-dial phone, some with airconditioning, some reserved for non-smokers. **Facilities** Elevators, restaurant (with no-smoking areas), bar, lounge, private dining rooms, safe-deposit boxes, champagne teas, afternoon snacks, residents' after-theater suppers, same-day cleaning/laundry/pressing. **Restrictions** Dogs by arrangement only. **Terms** Expensive. Some weekend special breaks. **Lunch** Expensive; expensive fixed-price menu. **Dinner** Expensive; expensive fixed-price menu. **Credit cards** All major cards. **Nearest tube station** Green Park, 300 yds. **Hotel parking** No. NCP in Carrington Street, W1 (Shepherd Market), hotel will take car to and from car park for small charge. **Local eating** The Ritz (see p. 77); Fortnum and Mason's and Simpson's, Piccadilly; The Connaught (see p. 37); Westbury Hotel, Conduit Street, W1. **Local shopping** Bond Street, Piccadilly stores; Jermyn Street; Burlington Arcade; Cork Street commercial art galleries; Regent Street stores. **Local interest** Royal Academy; Museum of Mankind; Green Park and Buckingham Palace.

11 Cadogan Gardens

A stylish town house

Staying at 11 Cadogan Gardens is like visiting very English, very aristocratic friends who have unavoidably been called away, but have kindly left you the use of their fully staffed house in town. From the outside there is nothing to indicate that this gabled, red-brick mansion is other than a private residence. Ring the bell and a porter in a stiffly starched white jacket instantly appears to take your suitcases. You are greeted in the oak-panelled hall, which has beautiful arrangements of fresh flowers, and you sign the Visitors' Book. Kind enquiries are made as to whether you would perhaps like a cup of tea, a sandwich, or light meal. An elevator carries you up past the oak-bannistered staircase, whose walls are hung with portraits in oils, and you are guided through a series of corridors to your room. Having made certain that it is to your satisfaction, enquired the hour at which you wish breakfast to be brought to you, and encouraged you to leave your shoes outside the door at night to be polished, the management leaves you in peace.

Do not expect designer décor, though bathrooms have been revamped. In the way that all connoisseurs of the English way of life will instantly recognize and appreciate, excellent antiques, quite ordinary oak and mahogany furniture, elegant fabrics, cozy chairs, charming Victoriana, and plenty of magazines and books are assembled as in a family home. There is a formal drawing room, but no dining room. The range of bedrooms includes tiny single rooms, small suites, and some enormous double rooms. The splendid Garden Suite has its own door on to the street, two vast bedrooms, a huge drawing room with elaborate fireplace and club fender, and an air of sedate distinction that makes it eminently suitable for the international antique dealers by whom it is often selected.

In the morning, breakfast trays rattle up from the kitchens below in the dumb waiter. Breakfast is well presented, with heavy linen napery, a large glass of freshly squeezed orange juice, fresh fruit, croissants, a large jug of excellent coffee, and, if you wish, kippers or bacon and egg. Room service offers home-made light snacks and afternoon tea.

Arrangements can be made for visits to hairdresser, theater, or restaurant. The Rolls and Roy the chauffeur are at your disposal for journeys to and from the airport, or for sightseeing or shopping expeditions. On a fine day a porter will carry a deckchair into the private garden for you to sit in peaceful, leafy tranquility. On leaving, you will stop at the manager's office to settle your account, and to leave something for the staff, since direct tipping is not customary here. A stay at 11 Cadogan Gardens is a memorable experience.

The interiors have an elegant domestic atmosphere: there are pretty fabrics in the bedrooms (above), antiques in the sitting room (opposite, bottom), and oil paintings on the stairs. The exterior view is from Cadogan Gardens.

---

11 CADOGAN GARDENS, Sloane Square, SW3 2RJ. **Map reference** 7. **Tel.** (01) 730 3426. **Telex** 8813318. **Fax** (01) 730 5217. **Owners** 11 Cadogan Gardens Ltd. **Managers** Mark Fresson, Miss Claire Armstrong, Christopher Wallace. **Open** All year. **Rooms** 27 single, 29 double, 5 suites, all with bathroom, direct-dial phone, 30 with TV. **Facilities** Drawing room, elevator, safe, access to private garden, 24-hr. laundry and dry cleaning, conference/private dining room, chauffeur-driven Rolls or estate car. **Restrictions** No children under 10. **Terms** Expensive. **Lunch/Dinner** Room service only, home-made soups, salads, snacks, afternoon tea, etc., dinner parties by arrangement. **Credit cards** No, but travelers' checks and foreign currency accepted. **Nearest tube station** Sloane Square, ¼ mile. **Hotel parking** No. Nearest is under Carlton Tower Hotel, Cadogan Place, SW1. **Local eating** (All in SW3) snacks at L'Express and GTC, Sloane Street; Le Metro and The Capital, Basil Street (see pp. 55 and 27); Ma Cuisine, 113 Walton Street; Waltons, 121 Walton Street; The English Garden, 10 Lincoln Street; La Tante Claire, 68 Royal Hospital Road; La Poissonerie de l'Avenue, 82 Sloane Avenue. **Local shopping** King's Road boutiques, GTC, Sloane Street; Peter Jones, Sloane Square; Harrods and Knightsbridge stores. **Local interest** Chelsea Hospital and gardens (annual flower show in May); Chelsea Physic Garden; National Army Museum; Royal Court Theatre; King's Road.

Gourmet sophistication

The Capital is a gem. Hidden snugly down a quiet little street beside Harrods, in the heart of fashionable Knightsbridge, it has no vast echoing marble halls and no serried ranks of minions, but attentive porters appear at your taxi door when you arrive, and desk staff and managers are both welcoming and efficient. The hotel's Edwardian wing was once Squires Hotel, which flourished in the 1920s. Its wide and richly carved staircase, hidden away behind the snug little dark green sitting room, ascends to a maze of narrow corridors which lead to 10 bedrooms, all different in shape and size, with decor by the noted designer Nina Campbell, who created the elegant interiors for Hambleton Hall hotel in Leicestershire.

An elevator serves both this wing and another 45 rooms, individually redesigned by owner David Levin and his wife, Margaret. They have combined every thoughtful feature one would hope to find in a modern hotel with the beautiful fabrics, mellow wood, green plants, fresh flowers, paintings, and furniture one would expect only in an elegant private house. My airconditioned room in the Edwardian wing was furnished in creams and blues, with touches of terracotta. What seemed to be well-stocked library shelves opened to reveal a deep, walk-in, well-lit hanging and shelved closet, with extra storage space above for suitcases. The glamorous bathroom, most generously equipped with toiletries, had an excellent shower and towelling robes.

A new chef, Philip Britten, formerly with Chez Nico, creates delicately seasoned, elegantly presented dishes for the stylish restaurant. A terrine combining intricately interleaved sole and red mullet, on a light tomato coulis, tasted as good as it looked. Confit of duck in a rich red-wine sauce, tiny perfect vegetables,

a feather-light pear mousse sharpened with Poire William liqueur, and wispy *tuiles aux amandes* and chocolate truffles with the freshly-brewed coffee were all delicious. An informed choice of wines complements the superb cuisine. The restaurant is fashionable, so reserve a table when you book your room.

David Levin has turned the house next door to The Capital into six compact luxury apartments, complete with galley kitchens, and one door nearer to Harrods are L'Hotel and Le Metro (see p. 55), for those paying a rapid visit to London. His restaurant specializing in English dishes, The Greenhouse in Mayfair's Hay's Mews, completes a small empire which is the daily concern of its dedicated owner. He has created a happy *esprit de corps* among his staff, and a feeling of great contentment in his constantly returning guests.

Opposite: the hotel's beautiful restaurant is a famous rendezvous for gourmets. Above is one of the bedrooms designed by Nina Campbell; the bookshelves conceal closets.

THE CAPITAL, 22 Basil Street, SW3 1AT. **Map reference** 11. **Tel.** (01) 589 5171. **Telex** 919042 HOTCAP. **Fax** (01) 225 0011. **Owner** David Levin (Capital Hotels Knightsbridge Ltd). **Manager** Keith Williams. **Open** All year. **Rooms** In hotel: 12 single, 18 double, 15 junior suites; also 6 apartments and 1 studio; all with bathroom (including shower), color TV, direct-dial phone, airconditioning, mini-bar. **Facilities** Sitting room, bar, restaurant, 2 private suites for dinners, parties or meetings, 24-hr room service, same day laundry/valeting/dry-cleaning/pressing; baby sitting, secretarial service. **Restrictions** No dogs in public rooms. **Terms** Expensive. **Lunch** Moderate fixed-price menu. **Dinner** Deluxe. Expensive fixed-price menu. **Credit cards** All major cards. **Nearest tube station** Knightsbridge, 50 yds. **Hotel parking** Yes, 12 cars. NCP opposite hotel. **Local eating** (All in SW3) Le Metro, Basil Street (see p. 55); Waltons, 121 Walton Street; La Tante Claire, 68 Royal Hospital Road; La Poissonerie de l'Avenue, 82 Sloane Avenue. **Local shopping** Harrods and Knightsbridge stores; Sloane Street, King's Road, Brompton Road boutiques. **Local interest** Natural History, Science, Geological, and Victoria & Albert Museums; Royal Albert Hall; Hyde Park and Kensington Gardens; Kensington Palace.

A floating Victorian hotel

In 1875 Captain Webb became the first man officially recorded as swimming the English Channel unaided. He made many other record-setting swims along the Thames, which is why Paul and Gaynor Waterman felt it appropriate to name their 1890s Dutch-built barge after him.

This unique floating Victorian hotel has solid mahogany woodwork and is furnished with elegant bric-à-brac, comfortable settees, potted plants, and cane-seated chairs under a quilted silk ceiling. The open deck area, with flowering shrubs in pots, provides further space to laze about. The cabin bedrooms are modern, with excellent showers, constant hot water, ingenious and immaculate private facilities, flowered wallpaper, and fitted white furniture, including chests of drawers and hanging closets. Any extra baggage can be safely stowed aboard elsewhere. Firm, full-sized mattresses and cosy duvets ensure sound sleep.

You can wake to Windsor Castle glimpsed through the morning mist, framed in willow trees, take afternoon tea while snow-white swans drift slowly past in leafy Richmond, or watch the sun set over Greenwich Palace and the masts of teaclipper *Cutty Sark*. The boat moors at the foot of the Tower of London, and beside Hampton Court palace, where you can have an elegant private picnic in the Queen's Privy Garden, by special permission.

The atmosphere on board is more that of a house party than of a hotel. The twelve guests and six crew members are all introduced by Christian names only. There is an exciting feeling of all setting out on an expedition together, except that you sit back and are pampered, lingering over breakfast with the morning's papers, or chatting on the radio telephone while the crew neatly maneuver the boat through

amazingly engineered locks or prepare meals from fresh ingredients in the spotless modern galley.

Dinner on board, at a long table elegantly set and adorned with candles and fresh flowers, may include crab and asparagus mousse, Charles II's favorite fresh salmon in champagne with dill, and sweet nuts and peaches, a dish created to tempt the palate of Mary Tudor. The recipes were discovered by Gaynor in the libraries of the Thames-side palaces.

Groups of friends celebrating a birthday, anniversary, or reunion, or companies wishing to entertain clients, promote a product, or give employees an incentive treat, can charter private cruises in *Captain Webb*, Gaynor however reserving control of the menus. Those who enjoy boats, rivers, good food, and exploration will find life aboard *Captain Webb* both relaxing and fun.

Opposite: two views of the surprisingly spacious main cabin and a prospect of the Thames from the deck; Tower Bridge looms in the background. One of the boat's two friendly dogs is shown above. Overleaf: the full extent of the barge is revealed as it passes the Tower of London.

CAPTAIN WEBB, c/o Another Britain, White Cross, Water Lane, Richmond, Surrey. **Tel.** On board: (0836) 202408. **Telex** No. **Owners** Another Britain Co. **Managers** Paul and Gaynor Waterman. **Open** All year. **Rooms** 2 single, 2 double, 3 twin, all with private bathroom (no tubs, showers only), airconditioning and central heating. **Facilities** Cruises as arranged, available moored for dinner parties. Boat is 105 ft. long and 19 ft. 8½ in. wide. Open sundeck, sitting room, dining room areas, closecarpeted, with airconditioning and central heating, radio telephone, laundry by arrangement, bar, small library, complimentary morning papers. **Restrictions** None. **Terms** Expensive, but all meals and a champagne welcome, sherry, châteaux-bottled wines, buffet luncheons, afternoon tea, and

morning coffee are included. **Credit cards** All major cards, though personal checks are accepted. **Distance from transport** The ship moors beside places to be visited. Any more distant sightseeing is by complimentary taxi or small private coach. Arrangements are made to collect or deliver passengers from or to airport or hotel. **Local shopping/Local interest** A complimentary visit to the theater is generally included, and help and advice with ongoing shopping and touring is very expertly supplied. The highlights of the usual tour include Greenwich, Southwark Cathedral, the Tower of London, Hampton Court, and Windsor. There are also special interest trips; enquire when booking.

Claridge's

Magnificence revived

As in the story of the emperor who had no clothes, for the past few years nobody presumed to stand up and complain publicly about the growing shabbiness of Claridge's. How could anybody criticize what was virtually an annex of Buckingham Palace, praised by Queen Victoria in the 1850s, home from home for visiting kings, art deco gem of the 1930s with a tradition going back to 1812? Happily, England's most prestigious hotel has undergone a miraculous transformation under its new General Manager, Ronald Jones.

Nothing, heaven forbid, has been radically altered. But the liveried retainers, though stately and dignified as ever, have become once again attentive and concerned. The black-and-white marble floors shine, walls have been redecorated, carpets renewed, and the elaborately intertwined bronze heraldic shields gleam on the main staircase's sweeping balustrade. Air-conditioning has been unobtrusively installed in the famous restaurant, and in most of the bedrooms. The traditional mixture of priceless antiques, comfortable chairs, fine china, prints, elegantly carved fireplaces, statuary, and oil paintings remains unchanged, but spruced up. Those guests requiring their clothes to be unpacked, brushed and pressed, and their baths drawn to a specific temperature may have these services as impeccably performed as they would have been 170 years ago under the auspices of M. Mivert, French chef and first owner of the premises, or subsequently under Mr Claridge, former butler to the nobility.

When I arrived late one morning, ravenous, having left an unpleasant hotel after an uncomfortable night without stopping to eat, breakfast was upon request instantly wheeled in to my room. It was arranged on a starched gray linen cloth, and the delicious coffee was served in huge green and gold Wedgwood china cups decorated with a coronetted "C." The orange-juice was freshly squeezed, the croissants warm, and all, smilingly, at noon. My room, decorated with pretty sprigged paper, had enormous mirror-fronted hanging closets with towelling robes inside, a charming antique desk with dip-pen and inkwell, a color television, a supremely comfortable bed, and softest of down pillows. The fine linen sheets were changed when rumpled by my afternoon nap. An archway led to a gray marble bathroom with accessories beautifully set out on a white linen cloth, a huge bathsheet warming on a hot rail, and an excellent shower.

Dinner was highly enjoyable. Tempting *hors d'oeuvres* were followed by salmon trout with a sharp sorrel sauce, creamed spinach, and tiny new potatoes. Wild strawberries, coffee, and petits-fours completed an elegantly and courteously served meal. Ronald Jones has great pride in this historic building and his trust and confidence in his staff have inspired them. In such good hands, Claridge's is magnificent.

Opposite: Champagne and exotic fruit wait beside the bed of a fortunate guest. Above is a gleaming art deco interior; more 1930s splendor is shown overleaf (left). D'Oyly Carte's piano is preserved in the Royal Suite (right, top). The hotel's traditional English breakfast provides a hearty start to the day.

CLARIDGE'S, Brook Street, W1A 2JQ. **Map reference** 21. **Tel** (01) 629 8860. **Telex** 21872. **Fax** (01) 499 2210. **Owners** The Savoy Hotel plc. **Director and General Manager** Ronald Jones. **Open** All year. **Rooms** 53 single, 80 double, 57 suites, all with bathroom (including shower), color TV, direct-dial phone, radio. **Facilities** Restaurant, reading room, elevator, The Causerie Restaurant (smorgasbord restaurant at lunchtime, pre-theater and *à la carte* dinner), hairdresser, barber, flower/antique shop, 24-hour maid/waiter/valet service, Hungarian orchestra, safe. **Restrictions** Guide dogs only. **Terms** Deluxe. **Lunch/Dinner** (in restaurant) Deluxe. **Credit cards** All major cards. **Nearest tube station** Bond Street, 200 yds. **Hotel parking** No. NCP in Bourdon Street, W1. **Local eating** The Connaught (see p. 37); Scott's, 20 Mount Street, W1. **Local shopping** Bond Street; Cork Street commercial art galleries; young designer boutiques in South Molton Street; Regent Street (Laura Ashley, Jaeger, Liberty's); Burlington Arcade; Savile Row bespoke tailors and men's wear. **Local interest** Wallace Collection (art treasures); Wigmore Hall (concerts); Royal Academy; Museum of Mankind.

The Connaught

Exclusive grandeur

The Connaught remains unchangingly superb over the years. This exclusive hotel, just off Grosvenor Square and only a few steps away from the American Embassy, has a smartly uniformed doorman, instantly alert porters, and formal but welcoming desk staff. A series of elegant and comfortable but not overwhelming public rooms leads from the small central hall. Service is swift, attentive, and expert, and I had the impression of being the guest in some charming small palace or distinguished private residence rather than in a hotel. A solid oak staircase – or leisurely, period elevator – leads up to wide corridors, hung with huge oil paintings. Each bedroom has its own foyer, antique furniture, and splendid bathroom.

The food is magnificent and is served with great style. I thought it appropriate to invite to luncheon my husband's aunt, a grande dame, once lady-in-waiting to a now long-vanished royal court, and she pronounced The Connaught a survival of all that had been best in the luxury hotels she had known throughout Europe in the 1930s. Together we enjoyed quail eggs, served on an artichoke-based cream in a shell of meltingly light pastry, a dish of scallops, lobster, shrimps, and sole presented together in a perfectly seasoned sauce, followed by featherlight fresh strawberry mille-feuilles and delicious coffee. Dishes were presented for approval before being served, stiffly starched white tablecloths were changed by expert sleight of hand between courses without removing anything from the table, and the entire meal was of a quality that one would expect from a noted Michelin-starred chef. My bedroom had a rooftops view, and at night my bed was turned down, my nightclothes were laid out, and a small white linen mat was placed beside the bed, so that my bare feet would not encounter the carpet, a courtesy once current but now rare. In the morning, I

had only to touch one of the bedside bells for a smiling waitress to come to my door. She wrote down my breakfast requirements and reappeared five minutes later with a well-laden, linen-covered trolley. The valet, similarly summoned, bore away my suit for pressing and a maid went hurrying off to find a housekeeper, who instantly produced a hairdryer at my request.

Since The Connaught maintained its standards throughout a time when other hotels of similar character – now newly restored – were in decline, it has acquired a fiercely loyal clientèle who refuse to stay elsewhere. As a result it has become almost a private club, and guests book next year's visit during this year's and commend their friends to the manager. Should you wish to stay or have a meal here you must book very far ahead, and even then be prepared for disappointment.

Opposite and above: the imposing portico and stately façade on Carlos Place of this most aristocratically exclusive of hotels.

THE CONNAUGHT, Carlos Place, W1Y 6AL. **Map reference** 18. **Tel.** (01) 499 7070. **Telex** 296376. **Owners** The Savoy Hotel plc. **Managing Director and General Manager** Paolo Zago. **Open** All year. **Rooms** 17 single, 73 double, 24 suites, all with bathroom (including shower), color TV, direct-dial phone, radio. **Facilities** 24-hr. room service, Large Lounge, Small Lounge, restaurant, bar, Grill Room, elevator, safe. **Restrictions** Guide dogs only **Terms** Deluxe. **Lunch/Dinner** Deluxe. **Credit cards** Access only. **Nearest tube station** Bond Street, ¼ mile **Hotel parking** No. NCP under Britannia Hotel in Adam's Row, W1. **Local eating** Claridge's (see p. 33); The Greenhouse, 27a Hay's Mews, W1. **Local shopping** Bond Street; Burlington Arcade. **Local interest** American Embassy and Roosevelt Memorial, Grosvenor Square; Royal Academy; Museum of Mankind.

Dorset Square Hotel

A Regency retreat

The Dorset Square Hotel overlooks a pleasantly tree-filled square. This whole area was still open fields when in 1787 seven acres were fenced in by the enterprising Thomas Lord as a cricket ground. The Marylebone Cricket Club (MCC) was founded, and matches were regularly played, and reported in detail in the press. The rules of the game were somewhat more flexible then than now, it seems, for in 1802 an England side with 11 players is said to have played a team from Surrey of 22 players, and to have beaten them by 3 wickets. Monsieur André Jacques Garnarin, who made the first parachute jump from a balloon, took off from the cricket ground in 1802, in the presence of the Prince of Wales and "Persons of Fashion." In 1810 Mr Lord's lease expired, and taking the actual turf with him, he moved Lord's Cricket Ground to its present position in St John's Wood. In 1811 the area was developed, and a square was built where the cricketers had once played, named after a former patron of the sport, the Duke of Dorset.

The owner of the hotel has totally reburbished two of the charming Regency houses on one corner of the square, and converted another on the west side into spacious apartments. The entrance hall has a rack of antique cricket bats; the small sitting room containing the reception desk is strikingly furnished with a deep red settee and open fireplace, striped drapes, and masses of fresh flowers. There is a second equally delightful sitting room with an honor bar for residents only. Bedrooms have twice been individually refurbished since the hotel re-opened in 1986, and now have tasteful designer fabrics and antiques, Italian marble bathrooms with robes, excellent showers, and generous toiletries, and the convenient extras of mini-bar, remote-control TV, bedside phones, and large closets. My single room,

reached by a flight of stairs, was diminutive but sensibly priced. Furnished in pale yellow material with a large pattern of poppies, it had flower and landscape prints decorating the cream walls. I had a most comfortable overnight stay, followed by an excellent breakfast. Those staying longer should request one of the small double rooms, which have more space, or – for an even lengthier visit – one of the attractively furnished and very spacious apartments (one even contains a grand piano). There is a restaurant, recently delightfully painted with fantasy tree-houses. Since changes of chef are rumored, it would be wise to check the current status of the cuisine.

The Dorset Square Hotel, close to the splendid Regency terraces and flower-filled gardens of Regent's Park, has already established itself as a firm favorite with frequently returning guests.

Both the bedrooms and the public rooms (opposite and above) are most comfortably and elegantly furnished.

DORSET SQUARE HOTEL, 39/40 Dorset Square, NW1 6QN. **Map reference** 16. **Tel.** (01) 723 7874. **Telex** 263 964 DORSET G. **Fax** (01) 724 3328. **Owner** Timothy Kemp. **Manager** Bob de Bilt. **Open** All year. **Rooms** 6 single, 31 double, 12 apartments. Some rooms have airconditioning, all rooms and apartments have bathrooms (including shower), direct-dial phone, color TV, radio, minibar. Apartments also have video recorders and full 24-hr. room service. **Facilities** 2 sitting rooms, honor bar, restaurant, elevator. **Restrictions** None. **Terms** Expensive. **Lunch/Dinner** Moderate. **Credit cards** All major cards. **Nearest tube station** Marylebone, 50 yards. **Hotel parking** No. NCP in Marylebone Road, opposite hotel. **Local eating** The Connaught (see p. 37); Claridge's (see p. 33); Nanten Restaurant and Yakitori Bar (Japanese food), 6 Blandford Street, W1; Topkapi (Turkish food), 25 Marylebone High Street, W1. **Local shopping** Bond Street; Marylebone High Street. **Local interest** Wallace Collection; Planetarium; Wigmore Hall; Regent's Park and London Zoo.

In the heart of Chelsea

Neat steps lead up steeply to the front door of The Draycott, between two potted bay trees. There is no outward sign that this is a hotel, beyond a discreet small oval brass plate beside the front door. The gardens, in which guests may wander at will, are hidden away, enclosed by the houses of this 19th-century square, in a part of town popular with London's fashionable young. The Draycott was once, it is said, the home of Lord Cadogan. It later became the British Overseas Club, but fell into a gentle decline, from which it has been triumphantly rescued by Gordon Campbell Gray, owner also of The Feathers, a welcoming country retreat in Woodstock, near Oxford.

The Draycott's hallway is L-shaped, carpeted in soft green, panelled in white, and balconied. A fetching portrait of an Edwardian Countess gazes approvingly down at lovely arrangements of fresh flowers. There are deep comfortable armchairs and settees in the gracious drawing room, excellent antique furniture, and a fire in the hearth each evening. Light filters greenly in through the trees just outside the windows: one could be in the countryside.

I was the Draycott's first-ever visitor on its first evening as a hotel. Arriving a week ahead of Joan Collins and Robert Wagner, I spent a most comfortable night in a lavish four-poster, under a cream-lined, pink-rose-bedecked draped canopy, which echoed the deep pink of the settee. On the polished mahogany antique dressing table was a Chinese vase filled with fragrant pot-pourri, redolent of rosemary, blended by Harrods. Each of the bedrooms, which are mostly extremely spacious, has its own individual decor. Mine had prints and oil-paintings in antique frames, lacquered reading lamps, and *gros point* chair seats embroidered with roses. The original garlanded plasterwork remained

between the pretty wallpaper and high ceiling and I especially enjoyed being able to curl up on a settee in the firelight before the gas-coal hearth. The tiled bathrooms are modest in size, but well-equipped, with excellent showers.

There is no restaurant, but the young and attentive staff have a pleasing willingness to produce delicious light snacks and salads at any time from a room-service menu which also includes sausage and mash, BLTs, home-made soup, and rich chocolate cake. You may have if you wish a champagne breakfast or a lavish afternoon tea: even after midnight 24-hour room service ensures sustenance. Manager Sally Bulloch will advise on shopping and touring – she helped two guests track down a four-foot-high blue china elephant and an instantly-available private jet on one busy day just after the hotel opened. Spacious rooms, excellent service, elegant decor, tasty snacks, and a fashionable location will rapidly establish The Draycott as one of London's most exclusive hotels.

The quiet spacious bedrooms (opposite, above) look on to the gardens. One of the four-poster beds appears above. The beautiful sitting room (opposite, below) is decorated – like much of the hotel – with brilliant arrangements of fresh flowers.

THE DRAYCOTT, 24–26 Cadogan Gardens, SW3 2RP. **Map reference** 6. **Tel.** (01) 730 6466. **Telex** 914947 DRACT G. **Fax** (01) 730 0236. **Owner** Gordon Campbell Gray. **Manager** Sally Bulloch. **Open** All year. **Rooms** 6 single, 20 double, all with bathroom (including shower), direct-dial phone, color TV, radio, mini-bar, gas-coal fire. **Facilities** Drawing room, breakfast/conference room, elevator, garden, 24-hr. room service. **Restrictions** Dogs by arrangement only. **Terms** Expensive. **Lunch/Dinner** Moderate (snacks only). **Credit cards** All major cards. **Nearest tube station** Sloane Square, 250 yds. **Hotel parking** No. NCP in Sloane Street, SW3. **Local eating** (All in SW3) The Capital and Le Metro, Basil Street (see pp 27 and 55); Walton's, 121 Walton Street; Ma Cuisine, 113 Walton Street; La Tante Claire, 68 Royal Hospital Road; La Poissonerie de l'Avenue, 82 Sloane Avenue, SW7. **Local shopping** Harrods and Knightsbridge stores; King's Road boutiques; designer fashions in Sloane Street. **Local interest** South Kensington museums; Albert Hall; Hyde Park and Kensington Gardens

Dukes Hotel

A well-kept secret

The quality of Dukes Hotel can best be described as quiet excellence. More than at any other London hotel, to arrive at this privately owned, exclusive, and elegant establishment gives the impression of coming home to one's own very grand and very well-run mansion. Perhaps this is because it is in a tiny cul-de-sac off an already quiet street leading from St James's and has its own private courtyard, full of flowers and still gas-lit at night. Perhaps it is because of the lack of fuss about all the services provided. The 36 bedrooms and 22 suites are simple, but handsome and scrupulously maintained and great snowy heaps of huge white bathsheets are kept warm on hot rails in the impeccable marble bathrooms. The only word of complaint I have heard in many years of knowing Dukes was about the bedrooms' generally modest size, but now even this has been rectified by enlarging those on the upper floor. Suites have also been redecorated in antiques and pretty designer chintzes.

The reception rooms, with patterned plaster ceilings, have kept their charmingly Edwardian character. It takes only a glance and a quiet word instantly to produce a drink, a tray of teatime goodies, or a mouth-watering menu as you sit in the small panelled bar, furnished with leather chairs and hung with ducal portraits, or in the cosy little drawing room, or in the tiny alcoved dining room. By some magic, I have never found any of the public rooms, or indeed the hallway, uncomfortably crowded.

Dukes has an excellent young British chef, Tony Marshall, and an appetising menu includes quail and lobster, a choice of vegetarian dishes, and both exotic and traditionally British desserts. I enjoyed artichokes filled with ratatouille in puff pastry, poached wild salmon with faultless hollandaise, a smooth mango sorbet, and rich chocolate truffles with the delicious coffee. Diners can enjoy a famous selection of brandies and armagnacs in the bar (some date back to 1812). At lunchtime there is a most tempting *table d'hôte*. Softly lit at night, with particularly pleasant, unobtrusive, and faultless service, Dukes restaurant is a delight.

A house has stood here since Charles II's time, but was rebuilt in 1895 as chambers for the sons of the nobility. Although it became a hotel in 1908, Dukes has never lost the atmosphere of a private residence, from which one may stroll across to the ancient little St James's shops to be measured for hand-made shirts, shoes, or hats, or go down to the flowery gardens of St James's Park. As the hotel likes to say, Dukes is one of London's best-kept secrets.

Opposite: a corner of one of the delightful bedrooms (top) and the panelled bar. The food (above) is especially notable.

DUKES HOTEL, 35 St James's Place, SW1A 1NY. **Map reference** 27. **Tel.** (01) 491 4840. **Telex** 28283. **Fax** (01) 493 1264. **Owner** Dukes Hotel Ltd. **Managing Director** Richard Davis. **Open** All year. **Rooms** 8 single, 28 double, 16 suites, all with bathroom (including shower), direct-dial phone, TV, radio. **Facilities** Drawing room, bar, dining room, elevator, 1 small and 1 large function room, secretarial service, same-day laundry/drycleaning/valeting/pressing service, 24-hr. room service, safe. **Restrictions** Children under 8 by arrangement only; no dogs. **Terms** Deluxe. **Lunch/Dinner** Deluxe. **Credit cards** All major cards. **Nearest tube station** Green Park, $\frac{1}{4}$ mile. **Hotel parking** No. NCP in Arlington Street, SW1. **Local**

eating Fortnum and Mason's and the Royal Academy, both in Piccadilly, for light meals; Suntory, 72 St James's Street, SW1; Le Caprice, Arlington House, Arlington Street, SW1; Wilton's, 55 Jermyn Street, SW1; The Ritz (see p. 77); The Stafford (see p. 87). **Local shopping** Jermyn Street for menswear, and English perfume at Floris; auctions at Sotheby's and Christie's; Burlington Arcade; Fortnum and Mason's, Simpson's, Hatchard's (books), Piccadilly; Burberry's, Haymarket. **Local interest** Royal Academy; Museum of Mankind; Design Centre, Haymarket; National Gallery and National Portrait Gallery; St James's Park, Green Park, and Buckingham Palace.

Ebury Court

Civilized simplicity

It is highly unusual to come upon a London hotel that has been under the same owner-management for 50 years, but then Ebury Court is not a usual hotel. It belongs to Diana Topham, once a pupil at Cheltenham Ladies' College, and her husband, Romer, formerly a barrister of Lincoln's Inn. Since it is a home – their daughter was raised here and other members of the family have helped out in times of crisis – it has a specially domestic and very British atmosphere that is much appreciated by country gentry and visiting anglophiles alike. The same guests have returned so often that they have their own private clubroom and bar; drinks are brought to other visitors upon request.

The hotel occupies a graceful row of five small houses that was being built while Queen Victoria and Prince Albert were raising their large family half-a-mile away in Buckingham Palace. The mood is civilized, fairly formal, but warm and welcoming. A restaurant with cozy alcoves and low ceilings has been created in what were once cellars and store rooms. The food is the best sort of traditional home cooking, with sausages from the Queen's supplier, bread baked every day to a recipe given to Mrs Topham by a nun, and beef from Scotland. The 39 delightful small color-washed bedrooms are not for those travelling with large amounts of heavy luggage, or seeking self-indulgent luxury. Much of the furniture is plain, and painted white; the hanging closets are tiny, but the chests of drawers provide useful extra space. Bathrooms are *en suite* wherever the mid-1800s architecture allows; where it does not, they are a short walk down the corridor. Some have showers. Possessions accumulated over the years include the family Hepplewhite four-poster; a wing chair and grandfather clock which belonged to Romer's father, Judge Topham; a genuine featherbed that needs the porter's help to turn; porcelain hand-painted door

knobs; and some good antiques. Bedlinen is crisp and there are lovely chintzes.

Arriving hot and exhausted for lunch, unbooked, at the height of the tourist season, and at nearly two in the afternoon, I was warmly welcomed and a seat was found for me in the restaurant. I was made to feel special though I had never set foot there before, and this impression was reinforced when I returned to stay. Ebury Court is not designer decorated, but has the comfortably lived-in and loved feeling of the family house that it is. Winner of the prestigious César Award from the *Good Hotel Guide* for "maintaining old-fashioned hotel virtues in the metropolis," it embodies – like its kindly, unobtrusive, and gracious owners – all that is best in Britain.

The prettily draped four-poster bed opposite and attractive antique writing desk above are typical of the old-world charm of this friendly hotel.

EBURY COURT, 26 Ebury Street, SW1 W0LU. **Map reference** 8. **Tel.** (01) 730 8147. **Telex** No. **Owners** Romer and Diana Topham. **Open** All year. **Rooms** 22 single and 17 double, of which 11 have bathrooms (some with showers); all have radio and phone. Color TV can be hired. **Facilities** Elevator, sitting room, writing room (with TV), club bar, restaurant, safe, pre-theater suppers available from 6.30 pm. **Restrictions** No children under 5 in restaurant. **Terms** Moderate (English breakfast included). **Lunch/Dinner** Moderate. **Credit cards** Access/Visa. **Nearest tube station** Victoria, 100 yds. (NB Victoria rail station provides direct link to Gatwick Airport). **Hotel parking** No. NCP in Semley Place, SW1. **Local eating** Ciboure, 21 Eccleston Street, SW1; The Goring Hotel (see p. 51); The Berkeley (see p. 15); Memories of China, 67–69 Ebury Street, SW1. **Local shopping** Army and Navy Stores, Victoria Street. **Local interest** Buckingham Palace (Royal Mews and Queen's Gallery are open to the public); St James's Park; Green Park; Westminster Abbey and (RC) Cathedral.

Orchids and champagne

It is fitting that Fortyseven Park Street should choose an orchid as its symbol. The marble entrance hall of this luxurious establishment leads, by elevator or graceful curving staircase, to 54 Edwardian-style high-ceilinged suites, built in the 1920s. Continental elegance has been combined with transatlantic understanding. Your morning coffee and croissants, or eggs and bacon, are brought to you by a staff with charming French accents; Continental white-linen-covered, down-filled duvets are on the beds; champagne and a vase of delicate orchids await your arrival, courtesy of the management. Each peaceful, triple-glazed and airconditioned suite has a gleaming marble bathroom with soft Christy towels and robes, and an efficient shower; those on the top floor have yew-wood furniture. Bedrooms are uncluttered, with good mirrors and well-placed lighting, and ample hanging space for clothes. There are push-button direct-dial phones in both bedroom and sitting room, comprehensive mini-bars, large remote-controlled color televisions, and a well-equipped all-electric galley kitchen, which will be fully stocked should you so request.

Fortyseven Park Street has no restaurant of its own, but it adjoins Le Gavroche, London's only Michelin three-star restaurant, domain of Albert and Michel Roux, from where delicious light meals from a room-service menu can be sent up to you directly. Should you wish to eat in the restaurant, it is as well to make your reservation when booking your room, since tables are always very much in demand. A private door leads from the hotel into Le Gavroche. Meals here are an event. The low-ceilinged, dark-green dining room gleams in the candlelight with polished silver and shining glassware, and has a profusion of beautifully arranged fresh flowers. The service is impeccable. The wine list, which contains only the best vintages of the best wines, is a connoisseur's delight and the menu, in French only, is adventurous and creative. I found the soufflé suissesse, a light cheese soufflé daringly flipped over while cooking, and served with a creamy sauce, delicious, though I query serving madeira sauce with the otherwise delectable seabass and salmon-trout. Perfect apricot icecream, a large dish of freshly made petits-fours, and excellent coffee completed a most memorable meal.

Fortyseven Park Street is run by manager Keith Bradford with polished expertise and charm. Just off Park Lane, in the heart of Mayfair, and only a short distance from the American Embassy, it is an ideal base for several days in London's most exclusive residential area.

Opposite is the main staircase, with splendid stained glass; above is a marble bathroom. Overleaf: left, champagne for two in an apartment and the famed restaurant Le Gavroche, which adjoins the hotel; right, a charming pastel-painted bedroom.

FORTYSEVEN PARK STREET, 47 Park Street, W1Y 3HD. **Map reference** 19. **Tel.** (01) 491 7282 (Le Gavroche: (01) 408 0881). **Telex** 22116 **Fax** (01) 491 7282. **Owners** Fortyseven Park Street Ltd. **General Manager** Keith Bradford. **Open** All year. **Rooms** 52 twin-bedded suites, with 1 or 2 bedrooms, all with sitting room, bathroom (including shower), kitchen, direct-dial phone, airconditioning, safe. **Facilities** Elevator, room service, 24-hr. reception, maid service, key-card security, same-day laundry/dry-cleaning service, secretarial service, theater bookings, safe; private reception suite with dining room, cocktail lounge and meetings room. **Restrictions** No dogs. **Terms** Deluxe. **Lunch/Dinner** (in Le Gavroche) Deluxe. **Credit cards** All major cards. **Nearest tube station** Marble Arch, ¼ mile. **Hotel parking** No. NCP in Park Lane, W1, or parking in Selfridge Hotel, Orchard Street, W1. **Local eating** The Greenhouse, 27a Hay's Mews, W1; The Connaught (see p. 37); Scott's, 20–22 Mount Street, W1; **Local shopping** Bond Street; Burlington Arcade; Piccadilly stores; Cork Street commercial art galleries. **Local interest** Wallace Collection; Royal Academy; Museum of Mankind; Wigmore Hall; Hyde Park.

Beside Buckingham Palace

Should you wish to call officially upon the Queen, or attend a royal garden party, you will find The Goring very convenient. It is in a quiet side street beside Buckingham Palace, just round the corner from the Royal Mews, so that the carriage sent for distinguished visitors can wait in front of the hotel's main door without holding up the traffic and will then have only a gentle half-mile for the horses to trot to reach the palace's main gates. When any large official occasion is in progress the hotel is always in demand as an honorary extra wing to the palace. This is a role it fulfils with distinction, for it is a handsome Edwardian building, immaculately kept, the outside decorated with flowering windowboxes. The stately entrance hall has a black-and-white marble floor; the friendly reception staff are especially efficient. Beyond is a spacious and comfortable lounge and bar which look into a central garden whose neatly trimmed lawns and tidy flowerbeds cover an area once crammed with notorious slum houses.

The first Mr Goring built his hotel in 1910 in what was then an unfashionable area, forseeing the demand there would be for accommodation for passengers to the Continent setting off from nearby Victoria Station, then approaching completion. It is still a family hotel, run by the grandson of the founder. Many of the staff have served succeeding generations, and, like family retainers, are extremely concerned about the comfort and care of the guests.

In the welcoming restaurant, waiters solicitously ply you with generous helpings of roast meats, delicious fresh vegetables, and succulent desserts from a menu which has both splendidly traditional and innovative dishes. The bedrooms, many recently redecorated, are either wood panelled and traditional, or fresh and chintzy. Mine had a brass bedstead, pretty peach-pink easy chairs, a desk, and a substantial range of Edwardian fitted cupboards.

Bathrooms, mostly reburbished in marble and mahogany, have excellent showers.

The hotel's history is well documented in a book by the first Mr Goring's son, which can be purchased here. It is not only monarchs and their entourages who appreciate the old-world courtesy and traditional comforts of the hotel. Any of its guests will tell you that "they really look after you at The Goring."

Portraits of the Goring family and photographs of their staff are proudly displayed in their hotel (above). Opposite is a pretty chintzy bedroom. Overleaf: left, a stairway topped by a flamingo; right, a view of the grassy square on to which the hotel backs, and one of the colorful windowboxes that brightens the façade.

THE GORING HOTEL, 15 Beeston Place, Grosvenor Gardens, SW1 WoJW. **Map reference** 15. **Tel.** (01) 834 8211. **Telex** 919166. **Fax** (01) 834 4393. **Owner** George Goring. **General Manager** William Cowpe. **Open** All year. **Rooms** 38 single, 45 double, 7 suites, all with bathroom (including shower), color TV, radio, direct-dial phone. **Facilities** 24-hr. room service (sandwiches and beverages only from 10.30 p.m. to 7.30 a.m.), elevator, restaurants, sitting room, bar, 5 private dining rooms, safes, same-day laundry/dry cleaning/valeting/shoe cleaning and mending services. **Restrictions** No dogs. **Terms** Expensive. **Lunch/Dinner** Expensive. **Credit cards** All major cards. **Nearest tube station** Victoria, 100 yds. **Hotel parking** Yes, in mews opposite by arrangement (capacity 12 cars). **Local eating** Ciboure, 21 Eccleston Street, SW1; La Tante Claire, 68 Royal Hospital Road, SW3. **Local shopping** Army and Navy Stores, Victoria Street. **Local interest** Buckingham Palace; St James's Park; St James's Palace; Westminster Abbey and (R.C.) Cathedral.

L'Hotel

French Provincial chic

Step through the rather grand marble doorway of L'Hotel, and you seem to have entered some delightful French country hotel, or rural New England Inn. The hall is wide and full of light, there are green plants, sisal matting on the floor, a wooden dresser with a row of white china hens, cream-colored walls stencilled faintly with wild roses and sheaves of corn, and a handsome stripped-pine desk behind which sits one of the staff, waiting to greet you. Enchanting modern primitive paintings of sheep and cattle against a background of bright blue sky and emerald grass hang on the walls. A staircase with splendid oak bannisters leads up past hanging antique quilts to 12 rooms with red-baize-covered, brass-studded doors, and down – past enlargements of *premier cru* wine labels – into Le Metro, the wine bar in the cellar.

The bedrooms are simple, but extremely civilized. Each has a pine desk and chair, a free-standing pine wardrobe, a Windsor chair, and a brass bedstead with fine linen sheets. There are pretty tiles in the good modern bathrooms, which have a tub and hand-shower. Mrs David Levin has deliberately kept L'Hotel's furnishings simple, since those who want more elaborate décor as well as more pampering service have the alternative of The Capital hotel next door, also owned by her husband (see p. 27). With the busy and independent in mind, there is no room service; you are given the key to the front door, and the staff leaves at 6.00 p.m. In emergency you can, of course, always call on The Capital.

A splendid breakfast is served downstairs in Le Metro, which is also open to non-residents. The staff are here early in the morning, bustling about in their long white aprons to bring you delicious coffee in huge green and gold cups, hot fresh croissants and crunchy rolls, with plenty of unsalted French butter and home-made preserves – all included in the price of the room. Bentwood chairs, tables with curly wrought-iron legs, an attractive bar, posters, and original sketches and cartoons on the walls add to Le Metro's charm and there is a tiny courtyard at the back with climbing plants on a trellis. A well-selected range of excellent-value wines are available by the glass or by the bottle. The food is both delicious and reasonably priced. Jambon persillé, salade frisée, and a tarte aux fraises simply heaped with fresh strawberries were memorable.

L'Hotel came into being when hotelier David Levin acquired the then rather rundown little turn-of-the-century hotel from its somewhat eccentric lady owner and removed layers of wallpaper and paint to show the fine wood beneath. L'Hotel is now spruce and immaculate, a perfect (and competitively priced) Knightsbridge pied-à-terre.

The bedroom above is typical of L'Hotel's delightfully simple interiors. Opposite: a corner of one of the bedrooms and a mouthwatering breakfast from Le Metro; the group of naive pictures of farm animals hangs in the foyer.

L'HOTEL, 28 Basil Street, SW3 1AT. **Map reference** 10. **Tel.** (01) 589 6286. **Telex** 919042. **Owner** David Levin. **Managers** Nicholas Cook and Joy Drinkwater. **Open** All year. **Rooms** 11 double (twin beds), 1 suite (double bed), all with bathroom (with tub and handshower), color TV, direct-dial phone. **Facilities** Le Metro wine bar in cellar, safe. **Restrictions** Dogs at discretion of management. **Terms** Moderate. **Lunch/Dinner** (in Le Metro) Moderate. **Credit cards** American Express, Visa. **Nearest tube station** Knightsbridge, 50 yds. **Hotel parking** No.

NCP opposite hotel. **Local eating** The Capital (see p. 27); Harrods, Knightsbridge, and L'Express and GTC, Sloane Street, SW1, for light meals; La Tante Claire, 68 Royal Hospital Road, SW3; Walton's, 121 Walton Street, SW3. **Local shopping** Harrods and other Knightsbridge stores; King's Road and Sloane Street boutiques. **Local interest** Hyde Park and Kensington Gardens; Royal Albert Hall; Natural History, Geological, Science and Victoria & Albert museums.

Hyde Park Hotel

Marble halls

Mounted Horseguards, breastplates gleaming, plumed helmets with chinstraps severely in place, horses burnished like polished metal, ride out from Knightsbridge Barracks past the Hyde Park Hotel several times a week. This imposing edifice was built in Victorian times as a set of elegantly furnished apartments for gentlemen. It became a hotel at the turn of the century, and in the 1920s Rudolph Valentino was a guest. In 1948 George VI and Queen Elizabeth celebrated their Silver Wedding here, but in the 1960s it fell into a decline, from which it has now been triumphantly rescued.

Everything about the Hyde Park Hotel is on a huge scale. A wide steep flight of white marble stairs leads up to more, now carpeted, stairs, and into a vast mirrored and pillared chandelier-hung foyer, its severe lines softened by immense arrangements of fresh flowers, trailing plants, and potted palms. The glorious Portuguese pink, Sicilian white, and Verdi dark green marbles of the foyer were uncovered in the course of restoration, after years beneath layers of dreary paint and wallpaper. Lofty archways lead through to a spacious sitting area, and on into the Park Room, which directly overlooks the green magnificence of Hyde Park. Here you can enjoy a leisurely English breakfast, excellent lunch, formally served afternoon tea, or candlelit dinner. Menus are based on fresh ingredients, now with some regional Italian specialities. The Drawing Room, newly reburbished, serves Ferrari champagne, a Business Lounge provides global communications even for non-residents: all innovations of dynamic manager Paolo Biscioni. Further reception rooms, a ballroom gloriously re-gilded in gold leaf, a glittering mirrored salon, the Park Suite, and the King Gustav Adolph Suite, favored by the late king of Sweden, have all been magnificently restored and are hung with Edwardian chandeliers. The dark-oak-panelled Grill Room has low ceilings, heavily embossed plasterwork, and, like the bar, the atmosphere of a club.

The bedrooms do not overwhelm. Known still as apartments, they are spacious and pleasingly proportioned and are furnished mainly with antique furniture; some have marvellous views of the park. The original hanging closets are large, the bedrooms' foyers have helpful extra space, there is good room service, a discreetly concealed mini-bar, and ultra-modern bathrooms with good showers. Overnight laundry, valeting, and drycleaning services are most helpful.

It is heartening to see the owners, Trusthouse Forte, whose hotels usually have far more modest pretensions, investing so many millions with such dazzling results.

A chandelier-hung staircase is shown opposite; above is one of the hotel's many views of leafy Hyde Park. Overleaf: left, an exceptionally elegant bedroom (top) and one of the suites; right, a private dining room (top) and the main staircase.

HYDE PARK HOTEL, 66 Knightsbridge, SW1 Y7LA. **Map reference** 13. **Tel./Fax** (01) 235 2000. **Telex** 262057. **Owners** Trusthouse Forte. **General Manager** Paolo Biscioni. **Open** All year. **Rooms** 14 single, 153 double, 19 suites, all with bathroom (including shower), direct-dial phone, color TV, radio, mini-bar, airconditioning. **Facilities** Elevators, restaurant, grill room, drawing room, bar, 24-hr. room service, laundry/dry cleaning/valeting service (including overnight service), hairdresser, conference facilities, theater ticket desk. **Restrictions** No dogs in public rooms. **Terms** Deluxe. **Lunch** Expensive Moderate fixed-price menu. **Dinner** Deluxe. **Credit cards** All major cards. **Nearest tube station** Knightsbridge, beside hotel. **Hotel parking** No. Nearest is in large garage serving hotel, for which fee is charged. **Local eating** The Capital (see p. 27); Le Metro, Basil Street, SW3 (see p. 55); L'Express, Harrods and GTC (Sloane Street, SW1), for light snacks. **Local shopping** Harrods and other Knightsbridge stores, including Harvey Nichols and Scotch House; Sloane Street boutiques. **Local interest** Hyde Park and Kensington Gardens; South Kensington museums; Royal Albert Hall.

Le Meridien

Splendor restored

Le Meridien has recently been totally reburbished. Close to Piccadilly Circus, it is within easy walking distance of many West End theaters and cinemas, Burberry's, Laura Ashley's, and Liberty's large stores, and the famous bespoke tailors of Jermyn Street. The interior is palatial. The vast magnificent Oak Room Restaurant has wood-panelled walls decorated with gilded trophies, garlanded leaves and flowers, helmets, swords, and shields in carved relief. Wonderful chandeliers, specially made in Italy, have wide swirling ribbons of glass and delicate crystal flowers glittering among the lights.

David Chambers, formerly of Dukes (see page 43), presides over the kitchens with the sure, delicate touch which I have always admired, and which has now won the Oak Room a coveted Michelin star. He has been newly inspired by visits to the kitchens of La Côte St Jacques, the noted restaurant in Joigny, France, whose owner, 3-star Michelin chef Michel Lorain regularly visits Le Meridien in London to create special menus based on his *cuisine créative* and *cuisine traditionnelle*. Famed dishes are his sea bass, lightly smoked, in a cream sauce with caviar, gazpacho with langoustines and quenelles of courgette, and his own boeuf bourguignon. The delightful glass-covered Terrace Garden Restaurant upstairs offers lighter fare among the greenery.

The bedrooms are all of different sizes, and long-stay guests with much baggage should request a capacious room. Refurbishments have gained top-rating classification for the air-conditioned, antique-furnished bedrooms with their lavish marble bathrooms. Champneys now run the health and fitness

complex beneath the hotel, and there is an international business communications center. A direct underground rail runs between Piccadilly and Heathrow. In the very capable hands of Air France, this stately old Edwardian hotel, on the edge of a revitalized Piccadilly, and a newly-respectable Soho, has finally regained its original *joie-de-vivre*.

The glass-covered Terrace Garden (opposite), overlooking Piccadilly, is the less formal of Le Meridien's two restaurants. The splendid chandelier above is in the gourmet Oak Room Restaurant. Overleaf is the imposing marble-floored entrance hall.

LE MERIDIEN, Piccadilly, W1V 0BH. **Map reference** 28. **Tel.** (01) 734 8000. **Telex** 25795. **Fax** (01) 437 3574. **Owners** Meridien Hotels (Air France). **Manager** Michel Novatin. **Open** All year. **Rooms** 98 single, 155 double, 31 suites, all with bathroom (including shower), air-conditioning, double-glazing, key-card security, color satellite TV, radio, minibar, hairdryer. **Facilities** 24-hr. room service, 2 restaurants, tea-lounge, safe, leisure complex (billiards room, lounge, coffee bars, squash courts, pool, sauna, jacuzzi, solarium, library, Turkish bath, nautilus gym, dance studio, beauty treatments). Business center with global communications, secretarial, translation, and interpreter services. Dry-cleaning/laundry/valeting/small repairs/valet parking services. **Restrictions** No dogs except guide dogs, by arrangement only. **Terms** Deluxe. **Lunch** Terrace Garden Restaurant: Moderate. Oak Room: Deluxe. Expensive fixed-price menu. **Dinner** Terrace Garden Restaurant: Expensive. Oak Room: Deluxe. Deluxe fixed-price menu. **Credit cards** All major cards. **Nearest tube station** Piccadilly Circus, 50 yds. **Hotel parking** No. NCP in Brewer Street, W1. **Local eating** Many small ethnic Soho restaurants; Dukes Hotel (see p. 43); The Ritz (see p. 77). **Local shopping** Piccadilly and Haymarket stores; Burlington Arcade; bespoke tailors of Jermyn Street and Savile Row; Bond Street and Regent Street stores. **Local interest** Close to many theaters and cinemas; Museum of Mankind, Royal Academy, National Gallery.

A Georgian mansion reborn

This is a hotel for those who like their history on the outside of the building and their modern comforts within. It stands in a lovely curved Georgian street built in 1789 and originally intended to be one half of a circular terrace, but the other half somehow never got built. The original porticoed façade and the 18th-century iron railings remain, beautifully maintained. The exterior is brightened by neat trees in tubs and windowboxes full of flowers. A welcoming doorman in dark brown and gold livery stands on the gleaming marble steps.

Once inside you are in a modern interior. The décor in the open-plan reception area, restaurant, and glittering bar is in the same soothing dark brown as the doorman's livery. Groups of extremely comfortable leather easy chairs and settees are scattered about, interspersed with large leafy plants in wooden pots, beautiful flower arrangements, and elegant antique desks for signing in. The total effect is sophisticated, yet pleasingly restful.

The whole hotel is climate controlled, a welcome luxury in English weather, and the bedrooms are pleasantly proportioned, without the claustrophobically low ceilings of many modern hotels. My single room had a queen-sized bed and military-campaign-style furniture, concealed in which were a large color television and a mini-bar. There was plenty of well-lit hanging and shelved space for clothes. Café-au-lait colored sheets, pale green walls, an apple-green carpet, and prints with touches of sharp pink formed an agreeable color scheme. I appreciated the built-in hairdryer, immaculate modern bathroom with many small extras, and the thick towelling robe.

The bedrooms at the front of the hotel have the original tall windows, but instead of making tall thin rooms the architect responsible for the conversion cleverly created delightful duplex suites. Each has a large comfortable sitting room, with ample space for entertaining, a fully-stocked bar, and an extra guest bathroom on the lower level. On the balcony above, reached by a charming wrought-iron spiral staircase, are the bed, hanging cupboards, and a larger bathroom. For the less spry there is a second entrance from the corridor at bedroom level.

The surrounding area has many pleasant Georgian houses and quiet squares, excellent chamber-music concerts in the Wigmore Hall, the world-famous Wallace Collection of armor, *objets d'art*, and paintings, and for shopping there is Selfridges practically on the doorstep. Traditional afternoon tea, with freshly-made finger-sandwiches, scones and cream, pastries and a choice of select teas, is now graciously served in the lobby. This is a hotel which knows how to combine convenience with period charm.

Opposite: one of the antique reception desks; above: the Georgian portico and the hotel's doorman.

THE MONTCALM, Great Cumberland Place, W1A 2LF. **Map reference** 20. **Tel.** (01) 402 4288. **Telex** 28710 MONTCM G. **Fax** (01) 724 9180. **Owners** Nikko Hotels Ltd. **General Manager** Jonathan Orr Ewing. **Open** All year. **Rooms** 27 single, 73 double, 12 suites, all with bathroom (including shower), color TV, direct-dial phone, radio, airconditioning, hairdryer, mini-bar (full bar in studios). **Facilities** Restaurant, foyer sitting area, bar, elevator, 24-hr. room service, laundry/dry cleaning/valeting/shoe mending services (same-day service on weekdays), baby sitting, safe. **Restrictions** Small dogs only, and by arrangement. **Terms** Deluxe. **Lunch** Expensive (moderate fixed-price menu). **Dinner** Expensive. **Credit cards** All major cards. **Nearest tube station** Marble Arch, 50 yds. **Hotel parking** No. NCP in Great Cumberland Place, W1. **Local eating** The Connaught (see p. 37); **Local shopping** Bond Street; Oxford Street. **Local interest** Wallace Collection; Wigmore Hall; Hyde Park.

A very English home

Elizabethan maps show "the waye from Uxbridge to London," which led through the market gardens of Ealing, past infamous Tyburn, site of public executions, to Oxford Street. A pleasant six-and-a-half mile drive from the city center, Ealing developed little until the arrival in Victorian times of the railway. Early photographs show hansom cabs waiting beside Haven Green in front of Ealing Broadway station, on the same cobblestones where taxicabs now stand.

At the far side of the Green, in a quiet leafy street in a conservation area, is the trim, rose-covered Victorian villa where the Curry-Towneley-O'Hagans live. With the help of their two young sons they have transformed a once-neglected house with briar-patch garden into a gracious home. At the same time, Judith O'Hagan improved her knowledge of London history by taking a history degree, and her husband, Paddy, changed professions from stage and television actor to craft teacher at a local school, in order to spend more time with his family.

This is not a hotel as such; guests are welcomed as family friends, and reservations are essential. The bedrooms are comfortable, have duvets on the beds, and bathrooms with electric showers to outwit the eccentricities of Victorian plumbing. Lovely rugs embroidered by Judith's mother are scattered throughout the house, and among the many books on the shelves are several by her father, England's leading expert on donkeys. Judith's parents live on their own small Channel Island. Her grandfather, a peer, built and for many years was chairman of The Dorchester in Park Lane, currently closed for total refurbishment.

Judith is an expert cook, specializing in tempting traditional English breakfasts, which include honey from next door's bees. Dinner, if requested, is served by candlelight at the big polished table. Hot Stilton tartlets, turkey breast stuffed with herbs from the garden, home-made brandy-mousse icecream with sliced fresh strawberries and peaches were all excellent; the meal concluded with a selection of English cheeses, Judith's own handmade chocolate truffles, and delicious freshly ground coffee. Paddy O'Hagan, also with lordly antecedents – one cousin was page to the Queen – still sometimes appears on television, but he prefers entertaining his guests and working on the garden. The house is full of heirlooms gleaned from both sides of the family, enhanced by their own collection of pictures and prints. The O'Hagans are fascinating and thoughtful hosts, and their home provides a convenient base for trips to the stately houses and palaces that line the Thames, and to Oxford or Windsor, without the need to cross London.

Opposite: top, both inside and out, this quiet home has an air of welcoming tranquillity; bottom, pans gleam over the cooking range in the kitchen. Above: an antique lace fan makes an unusual decoration.

---

52 MOUNT PARK ROAD, W5 2RU. **Map reference** 29. **Tel.** (01) 997 2243. **Telex** No. **Owners** Paddy and Judith O'Hagan (NB affiliated Wolsey Lodge, In the English Manner: see p. 7). **Open** All year, except 23 Dec.–2 Jan. **Rooms** 2 twin, both with ensuite bathroom with power-boosted shower. **Facilities** Sitting room, ¾-acre garden. **Restrictions** No dogs; no children under 6; no smoking in bedrooms. **Terms** Moderate. **Lunch** No. **Dinner** On request only. Moderate (wine included). **Credit cards** Access/Amex/Visa. **Nearest tube station** Ealing Broadway, ¼ mile. **Hotel parking** Yes. **Local eating** Small English and ethnic restaurants as recommended by hosts. **Local shopping** Large modern shopping mall. **Local interest** Gunnersbury Park (Rothschild mansion); Osterley Park and Syon Park (18th-cent. mansions); Ham House; Royal Botanical Gardens, Kew; Chiswick House; Marble Hill House; Hogarth's House; Heritage Motor Museum; Living Steam Museum; Musical Museum; Richmond Park; Hampton Court palace.

Number Sixteen

An art collector's delight

When I first set foot in Number Sixteen, I was not a guest. I arrived in Sumner Place exhausted, in a downpour on a hot day, with too much luggage, to stay in the hotel on the other side of the road, only to find that it was hidden by scaffolding. Bewildered by a series of unmarked doors with their doorbells disconnected, I struggled into Number Sixteen to throw myself on their mercy. They were sympathetic, welcoming, and amused, pointed out to me the correct entrance, and encouraged me to leave my suitcases with them until I had sorted out my problems. Returning later to stay, I therefore felt myself among friends.

Sumner Place is a perfect early Victorian street of graceful white-painted houses with pillared porticos. At one end there is bustling Old Brompton Road, with small useful shops, passing taxis, a post office, and an underground station with a direct link to both Heathrow and central London; at the other end is quiet, leafy Onslow Square.

Number Sixteen actually consists of four houses – numbers fourteen to seventeen. Their little back gardens are combined in one prize-winning, flowery display, overlooked by a conservatory. Michael Watson, the original owner, now involved only as an advisor, greatly enjoyed restoring these delightful houses, linked together on each floor by corridors which form galleries for the charming collection of pictures and prints he acquired while hunting down exciting wallpapers, antique furniture, bathroom fittings, bibelots, and bedcovers. All the rooms are different sizes and shapes and all have their own ensuite bathrooms which have been most ingeniously fitted in as space allows. Each bedroom has its own name and décor. "The Navy Room," for instance, has navy-blue walls, a hand-painted wooden sign from The Armada pub in Portsmouth, prints of sailing ships, and natutical memorabilia. All but two rooms can be reached by elevator – mine, "Yellow," had a yellow waffle-pattern Welsh Weaver bedcover and a hopeful pot of yellow begonias which harmonized with the furnishings, an agreeable mixture of antique and modern.

The hotel is staffed mainly by cheerful foreign students, as though by the offspring of a large friendly family. Only breakfast is provided, served in the bedrooms as there is no dining room, and kept deliberately simple in order that it can arrive exactly on time for those with appointments to keep. Every bedroom has a good list of recommended neighborhood restaurants, and there is an inhouse bar where guests help themselves and sign chits. Number Sixteen is an unpretentious but extremely civilized town-house alternative to London's more lavish hotels.

The graceful portico on Sumner Place (above) leads into elegantly furnished rooms filled with flowers and a choice collection of pictures (opposite and overleaf). The disgruntled stone dwarf is a feature of the well-tended, prize-winning gardens.

NUMBER SIXTEEN, 16 Sumner Place, SW7 3EG. **Map reference** 4. **Tel.** (01) 589 5232. **Telex** 266638. **Fax** (01) 584 8615. **Owner** Granfel U.K. Ltd. **Manager** Timothy Macdonald. **Open** All year. **Rooms** 33 double, all with bathroom (including shower), direct-dial phone, color TV, complimentary soft-drink mini-bar, hairdryer. **Facilities** Elevator, garden, conservatory, 2 sitting rooms, honor-bar, safe. **Restrictions** No dogs; no children under 12. **Terms** Expensive. **Lunch/Dinner** No. **Credit cards** All major cards. **Nearest tube station** South Kensington, 50 yds.

Hotel parking No. NCP in Sloane Avenue, SW3. **Local eating** La Tante Claire, 68 Royal Hospital Road, SW3; St Quentin, 243 Brompton Road, SW3; Walton's, 121 Walton Street, SW3; Hilaire, 68 Old Brompton Road, SW7; and see hotel's own guide. **Local shopping** Harrods and Knightsbridge stores; Walton Street boutiques. **Local interest** Natural History, Science, Geological, and Victoria & Albert museums; Royal Albert Hall; Hyde Park and Kensington Gardens.

The Portobello Hotel

Exuberant Victoriana

The Portobello Hotel is the brainchild of owners Tim and Cathy Herring and designer Julie Hodges. It combines two delightful late Victorian terrace houses which back on to a quiet communal garden – a happy green wilderness of tall leafy trees and untidy but colorful flowerbeds. I arrived during a children's summer party, with a brass band playing and excited children in party clothes scampering about the grass among picknicking adults; all marvellously in period, but, happily for sleeping jet-lagged guests, a rare occurrence.

Tim Herring's friends, experienced international travellers with minimal luggage, were weary of callous and boringly stereotyped hotels with unwanted trappings. They yearned for somewhere with personality, informal, civilized, caring, and comfortable, with food available around the clock and friendly faces to greet them. Not finding anywhere exactly right, Tim Herring and his team have created such a haven.

The hotel is a fantasy on a Victorian military theme. There is mahogany campaign furniture in the bedrooms and throughout the houses are intriguing antiques, huge mirrors, potted plants, military prints, and twirly cast-iron bannister rails. The tiny elevator has a fierce grill door that snaps shut like a mousetrap, the ceilings have elaborate plaster coves, and the tall windows are curtained in Household Cavalry scarlet cloth. The light-filled, cheerful basement bar and restaurant, for hotel guests only, has 24-hour service of salads, snacks, hot dishes, coffee, sandwiches, and drinks. Everything is tasty, if fairly basic, and is served with friendly informality.

Bedrooms vary greatly in size and furnishings, but are priced accordingly. Minute single rooms are as compact as ships' cabins. My full-sized bunk-type bed had a snow-white, down-filled duvet, a color television suspended over it, a direct-dial telephone on the bulkhead, a folding-out reading light, canvas captain's chair, and compact storage and hanging space. There is a concealed mini-bar, and a hot-water dispenser for the starter kit of tea and coffee. Continental or full breakfast is served either upstairs or in the basement. Refurbished bathrooms, lined in elegant brown-and-white tiles, some also with mahogany-panelled tubs, have shower stalls, mini wash-hand basins, and all other necessaries neatly stowed in ship-shape fashion. Double rooms have extra space and there are four exuberant suites – one with a round bed, draped with mosquito netting, and an amazing original free-standing bathtub, complete with many brass taps and complicated plumbing.

This is not a hotel for everyone, especially those much laden, but it is a wonderful find for independently-minded globe trotters, desperate for civilized takers of messages and guardians of mail and bored with fuss and flunkies.

Opposite: top, a tiny bedroom and the sitting room, its scarlet curtains reflected in an antique mirror; bottom, a table in the basement bar and restaurant. The hotel overlooks private gardens (above). Overleaf: left, one of the stylish suites; right, a view over trees from the hotel, and a four-poster bed.

THE PORTOBELLO HOTEL, 22 Stanley Gardens, W11 2NG. **Map reference** 1. **Tel.** (01) 727 2777. **Telex** 21879/25247 PORTO G. **Owners** Tim and Cathy Herring. **Managers** John Ekperigin, Fiona Amery. **Rooms** 9 single, 9 double, 7 suites, all with bathroom (including shower, 5 also with tub), direct-dial phone, color TV (suites also with video), mini-bar, hairdryer. **Facilities** Elevator (to 3rd floor only), sitting room, safe, 24-hr. bar/restaurant. **Restrictions** None. **Terms** Moderate. **Lunch/Dinner** Moderate. **Credit cards** All major cards.

Nearest tube station Notting Hill Gate, $\frac{1}{4}$ mile. **Hotel parking** No. NCP in Queensway, W2. **Local eating** Monsieur Thompson's, 29 Kensington Park Road, W11; Julie's and Julie's Bar, 135 and 137 Portland Road, W11. **Local shopping** Portobello Road and Kensington Church Street (antiques). Street market in Portobello Road on Saturdays. **Local interest** Architecture of Victorian crescents; Kensington Palace and Kensington Gardens; Holland Park. Neighborhood varies from very elegant to rather rough: the hotel will identify pleasant areas.

A château in Piccadilly

The Ritz is a marvellous gilded Louis XVI château in the heart of London, planted on prim Piccadilly, overlooking Green Park, and fronted by its own Parisian-inspired arcade of elegant shops. César Ritz, the famed Swiss hotelier who guided The Savoy Hotel in its early days (see p. 83), caused two smaller hotels to be demolished to make way for England's first steel-framed building, which even in 1906 cost more than a million pounds.

Walk through the Piccadilly entrance and you will find yourself among a glittering array of mirrors, chandeliers, ornate plasterwork, flowers, dark-pink velvet-covered chairs and draperies. Facing you is the opulent Palm Court, with gilded statuary and an assembly of small tables, couches, and chairs, where even hotel guests must book well in advance if they wish to take the fabled afternoon tea. Running the length of the hotel, parallel with Piccadilly, is the high-ceilinged promenade of the Long Gallery, which leads to one of London's most elegant and ornate dining rooms. Gilded swags of foliage looped beneath a painted ceiling are reflected in long mirrors. Tall windows overlook a terrace decked with flower-filled urns, beyond which is a small garden. Dinner at night in this Cinderella's ballroom is by the light of pink candles set on tables spread with pink linen cloths and adorned with pink flowers; the food is served on pink and white Royal Doulton china. Parma ham, freshly sliced, with melon ripe to perfection, lobster with a well-presented salad, tangerine sorbet smooth as silk, and coffee from an ornate silver pot crowned with a silver pineapple, accompanied by petits-fours, were all delectable. The comprehensive wine list includes some exceptional clarets and armagnacs. Next door is the private Marie Antoinette dining suite, a gilded and mirrored marvel.

My pale yellow and white painted bedroom had a huge antique mirror over an ornate marble mantelpiece, a yellow brocade cover on the extremely comfortable bed, big square down-filled pillows, and fine bedlinen laundered to perfect softness and embroidered with an ''R.'' All the hotel bathrooms are super-modern, placing efficiency before nostalgia. A delicious breakfast in bed was served on a tray with pretty blue china.

The hotel sparkles and is full of life; the service is excellent, both efficient and concerned. After a short stint in New York, that *enfant terrible* of the hotel world, Terry Holmes, formerly of The Stafford, is now Managing Director; he will certainly make the Ritz even Ritzier.

Opposite: teatime in the luxurious Palm Court; above: the hotel from Green Park. Overleaf: left, a drawing room and an example of the superb cuisine – breast of corn-fed chicken filled with a double mousse of crayfish and chicken, resting on a light crayfish sauce, with white and spinach-flavored fine noodles. Right, a spectacular staircase.

THE RITZ, Piccadilly, W1V 9DG. **Map reference** 24. **Tel.** (01) 493 8181. **Telex** 267200. **Fax** (01) 493 2687. **Owners** Cunard Hotels Ltd (Trafalgar House Group). **Managing Director** Terry Holmes. **Rooms** 15 single, 101 double, 14 suites, all with bathroom (including shower), color satellite TV, in-house videos, direct-dial phone, hairdryer, minibar; all with doubleglazing, some with airconditioning. **Facilities** 24-hr. room service, elevators, restaurant, Palm Court, Long Gallery, 3 private dining suites, ladies' and gentlemen's hairdresser, florist, kiosk. Same day laundry/drycleaning/valeting service. **Restrictions** No dogs (guide dogs excepted). **Terms** Deluxe. **Lunch** Expensive. Expensive fixed-price menus. **Dinner** Expensive. Expensive fixed-price menu. **Credit cards** All major cards. **Nearest tube station** Green Park, 20 yds. **Hotel parking** No. NCP in Arlington Street, SW1. **Local eating** Fortnum and Mason's and Royal Academy, Piccadilly, for snacks; The Stafford (see p. 87); Dukes Hotel (see p. 43). **Local shopping** Piccadilly stores; Burlington Arcade; Jermyn Street; Savile Row; Cork Street; Bond Street. **Local interest** Royal Academy; Museum of Mankind; Green Park and Buckingham Palace.

St James's Club

An art deco delight

Tucked away discreetly between The Ritz and St James's, the St James's Club is naturally as uncommunicative about its resident guests as any other leading London establishment. However, numerous distinguished guests followed in the footsteps of the original owner, Peter de Savary, and many also enjoy the club's sister establishments in Paris, on Los Angeles's Sunset Boulevard, and under Antiguan palms. When passing through London these glitterati frequently elect to stay at the St James's Club where, sheltered from the curious and autograph seekers, they will find their friends and colleagues, and enjoy the exclusive and lavish comforts of the distinguished late Victorian building which has been sumptuously transformed by an inspired Italian design team.

The club's restrained opulence is a variation on the late 1920s art deco style that flourished in Hollywood at its peak. Meticulously maintained, highly professionally managed, it has a welcoming bar in earth tones and leather and a reposeful restaurant with olive-green velvet benches, carved wooden chairs with dusty-pink upholstered backs, and charming line drawings after Erté. The service is excellent and the menu is composed with a real understanding of the needs of the world traveller. As is common in America, but so rare alas in London, it provides what the jet-lagged might actually want to eat and drink, rather than what the chef dictates and the wine waiter suggests. You can be served, with equal deference and attention, a magnum of Chateau Latour '59, smoked salmon, and roast duckling, or a simple meal of sausages and mashed potatoes.

The suites have high ceilings and shimmer with reflected light from the many mirrors. My room was

in café-au-lait and blues, the bedspread forget-me-not blue faintly patterned with tiny butterflies, and the plump settee was covered in gentian-blue velvet. Ladies travelling alone find fresh flowers waiting in their room, which already has toning arrangements of silk flowers. Each suite, from studio to penthouse, is different in size and shape, but all have excellent showers, well-stocked bars, ample storage space, and orchid-colored monogrammed sheets and towels. Doubleglazing and airconditioning ensure undisturbed slumbers. Carved in marble over the bath is a scallop shell, emblem of St James, and worn in medieval times by pilgrims to his shrine at Santiago de Compostela.

Now owned by the Norfolk Capital Group, the St James's Club is being refurbished, but its striking individuality will be maintained.

Opposite: a beautifully designed bedroom and a corner of the bar; above, a snooker table in the billiard room – note the cartoons on the walls.

ST JAMES'S CLUB, 7 Park Place, St James's, SW1A 1LP. **Map reference** 25. **Tel.** (01) 629 7688. **Telex** 298519. **Fax** (01) 491 0987. **Owners** Norfolk Capital Group Ltd. **Club secretary** Sarah Dawkins. **Rooms** 11 studios, 32 suites, 1 penthouse, all with bathroom (including shower), direct-dial phone, color TV, bar, radio. **Facilities** Elevator, library, restaurant, 24-hr. room service, secretarial facilities, bar, luggage storage and mail forwarding, small conference facilities, private dining, same day laundry and drycleaning, shoe cleaning and valeting, individual safes (but not in rooms). **Restrictions** After one visit, club membership must be sought before further stays. Club facilities are for members only. No dogs. **Terms** Deluxe yearly subscription. **Lunch/Dinner** Expensive. Moderate fixed-price lunch menu. **Credit cards** All major cards. **Nearest tube station** Green Park, 100 yds. **Hotel parking** No. NCP in Arlington Street, SW1. **Local eating** Dukes Hotel (see p. 43); Fortnum and Mason's, Piccadilly (light snacks); Suntory, 72 St James's Street, SW1; The Ritz (see p. 77); The Stafford (see p. 87). **Local shopping** Burlington Arcade; Piccadilly stores; Burberry's, Haymarket, for raincoats; Jermyn Street for hand-made shirts. **Local interest** Royal Academy; Museum of Mankind; St James's Palace; St James's Park; Buckingham Palace.

Palace by the Thames

For six centuries a building named The Savoy has stood on this site overlooking the Thames. The original long-vanished palace built by Peter of Savoy, uncle to Henry III, was said in Elizabethan times to have been "the fairest manor in England." Victorian entrepreneur Richard d'Oyly Carte, discoverer of Gilbert and Sullivan, built here firstly the still-existing Savoy Theatre, for presenting the famous operettas, then in 1889 a magnificent modern hotel, luxurious beyond belief, lighted by the new electricity. To it he tempted César Ritz as manager, the famed Escoffier as chef, and American millionaires, the crowned heads of Europe, the Prince of Wales, and all the beau monde as visitors. Whistler and Monet painted the Thames from its balconies, Johann Strauss's orchestra played here; Caruso sang; Pavlova danced. In the 1920s and 30s the décor was updated and the great liners brought filmstars from Hollywood with mountains of hatboxes and cabin trunks. The first Martini in the world is said to have beeen mixed in the American Bar, meeting place of London's expatriate American community. During World War II, The Savoy achieved the dubious distinction of being London's most bombed hotel; in the post-war austerity, business slumped.

But now new life has come to the historic Savoy, whose hotel school has trained many of the world's leading managers. The vast marbled and frescoed entrance hall bustles with activity, the restaurant overlooking the Thames, where the first Pêche Melba was created for singer Nellie Melba, gleams and glitters. Waiters in formal black tailcoats or starched white jackets whirl swiftly between tables, bearing food under domed silver covers. Afternoon tea in the Thames Foyer is justly famous – don't miss the freshly baked scones and self-indulgently creamy pastries. All the bedrooms have now been totally refurbished, with luxurious fittings and bathrooms, but the magnificent Edwardian Riverside Suites still remain for the nostalgia seeker. Antique-filled, painted in pastel colors, with plasterwork picked out in white, luxurious and spacious, they make an intriguing contrast with the 1920s rooms, which retain their original marble bathrooms. The Savoy is famous for its 12-inch-wide shower-heads that produce cascading tropical waterfalls. Breakfast arrives on a trolley, with starched cloth, a rose, the morning paper, and exquisite Wedgewood china. The hotel's own famous coffee, ground and vacuum-packed, may be purchased here and its own factories will make you a mattress, or your own monogrammed towelling robe.

The Savoy, revered, concerned, and majestic, carries on the traditions of the stately palace that once stood here.

Opposite: dinner is laid in a sumptuous private dining room; above, mirrors and marble fireplaces evoke Edwardian elegance in the suites. Overleaf: left, the hotel from the Embankment gardens; right, one of the sitting rooms and a supremely stylish bed.

THE SAVOY HOTEL, The Strand, WC2R 0EU. **Map reference** 23. **Tel.** (01) 836 4343. **Telex** 24234. **Fax** (01) 240 6040. **Owners** Savoy Hotel plc. **Managing Director and General Manager** Willy Bauer. **Open** All year. **Rooms** 57 single, 85 double, 49 suites, all with bathroom (including shower), color TV, direct-dial phone, radio. **Facilities** 24-hr. room service, waiter/valet/maid service, same-day laundry/drycleaning, elevators, restaurant, grill, American Bar, Upstairs Bar, Thames Foyer, 5 banqueting rooms, 8 salons, baby sitting, hotel car hire, safes, florist, ladies' and gentlemen's hairdresser, Heathrow office to assist arrival and departure, boutique, theater ticket desk, picnic hampers by special request. **Restrictions** None. **Terms** Deluxe. (Weekend breaks available.)

Lunch/Dinner (River Restaurant and Grill Room) Deluxe. River Restaurant has expensive fixed-price lunch menu and a fixed-price dinner menu which is expensive Sun.–Thurs. and deluxe Fri.–Sat. **Credit cards** All major cards. **Nearest tube stations** Embankment, Covent Garden, Charing Cross, Aldwych: all ¼ mile. **Hotel parking** Yes, for 500 cars. **Local eating** Boulestin, 1a Henrietta Street, WC2; Inigo Jones, 14 Garrick Street, WC2. **Local shopping** Covent Garden has numerous fashionable boutiques. **Local interest** Royal Opera House, Covent Garden; National Gallery and National Portrait Gallery; National Theatre and arts center on South Bank; Inns of Court and Royal Courts of Justice; Silver Vaults in Chancery Lane.

The Stafford

International renown

The Stafford is a lovely 19th-century mansion in a very quiet backwater off St James's. It has lofty public rooms embellished with ornate plasterwork, a devoted staff, many of whom have been here for anything up to 35 years, and an elaborately formal restaurant serving traditional French cooking. The menu disdains the simplicity of *nouvelle cuisine*; its dishes are rich in butter, cream, brandy, and eggs. Oysters are specially brought down from Loch Fyne, beef is from The Stafford's own Scottish herds, vegetables are perfectly cooked and served in generous helpings, desserts are deliciously rich, and everything is presented on embossed silver platters. There is even a choice of flambé dishes, served with a panache often sadly lacking elsewhere. Wines are from the hotel's deep cellars, said once to have belonged to nearby St James's Palace; beneath their whitewashed brick vaults specially-favored, often-returning guests hold occasional memorable reunions.

The heart of the Stafford is the American Bar, which is hung with trophies and pennants, caps, ties, cartoons, mounted antelope horns, flags, framed pictures and mementoes from guests who have come from all over the world. Many refuse to stay anywhere else in London, and have been returning for years, greeting the staff as old friends. Former manager Terry Holmes has moved across the road to The Ritz; his successor, David Ward, has a less ebullient management style, but has maintained the same high standards. The hotel is as always immaculate and service is rapid and courteous.

Just round the corner is the house in which Chopin stayed when he was in England to play his final concert; beyond it is St James's Street, which leads down to St James's Palace, the ancient red-brick royal residence built by Henry VIII, guarded by

ceremonially dressed soldiers marching formally up and down in front of its gates. A few steps beyond is St James's Park, once the hunting preserve of Queen Elizabeth I. Now flower-filled, its lakes bustle with wildfowl (including pelicans) and an ornate bandstand provides cheerful music to appreciative listeners comfortably seated in deckchairs; tree-shaded walks lead up to Buckingham Palace or across the park to Whitehall or the Houses of Parliament.

At the back of the hotel, hidden snugly away behind the bar, is a tiny garden terrace, where on summer days one may sit on the edge of the hotel's cobbled mews. Visitors relaxing from their transatlantic crossing are often to be seen enjoying the celebrated and delicious afternoon tea, which is served from silver pots and on dainty china. Nearly all the spacious bedrooms have been refurbished with fresh chintzes and their bathrooms modernized. The Stafford has its own blend not only of whisky but also of dignity, elegance, and a very warm welcome.

The sitting room and a private dinner party in the historic cellars are shown opposite; above is one of the spacious bedrooms. Overleaf is the welcoming American Bar, festooned with trophies brought by guests from all over the world.

THE STAFFORD, 16–18 St James's Place, SW1A 1NJ. **Map reference** 26. **Tel.** (01) 493 0111. **Telex** 28602. **Fax** (01) 493 7121. **Owners** Cunard Hotels Ltd (Trafalgar House Group). **General Manager** David Ward. **Open** All year. **Rooms** 11 single, 44 double, 7 suites, all with bathroom (including shower), color satellite TV, in-house videos, direct-dial phone. **Facilities** Restaurant, American Bar, 5 private dining rooms, Garden Terrace, 24-hr. room service, elevator, hotel driver/guide available. **Restrictions** No dogs. **Terms** Deluxe. **Lunch/Dinner** Deluxe. Expensive fixed-price lunch and deluxe fixed-price dinner menus. **Credit cards** All major cards. **Nearest tube station** Green Park, ¼ mile. **Hotel parking** No. NCP in Arlington Street, SW1. **Local eating** The Ritz (see p. 77); Duke's Hotel (see p. 43); Suntory, 72–73 St James's Street, SW1; Cecconi's, 5a Burlington Gardens, W1. **Local shopping** Bond Street; Jermyn Street; Burlington Arcade; Justerini & Brooks, St James's (royal wine merchants). **Local interest** St James's Palace; St James's Park, Buckingham Palace; Royal Academy

Stone House

Country hospitality in a charming town house

Just round the corner from one of London's most fashionable jewelers and silversmiths (patronized by the Princess of Wales), is a pleasant street of Regency houses. They had at one point rather come down in the world, but are now quite definitely up again. Area railings are freshly-painted, window-boxes overspill with colorful flowers, and Stone House waits to welcome guests.

The brass knocker recalls that of Oxford's Brasenose College; the narrow hallway, painted a deep peach, has been transformed into the image of an 18th-century print-room (with authentic prints), its size cleverly doubled by mirrors. A tiny reception area is squeezed in at the top of the first flight of stairs, and a few steps more take you to the drawing room and up again to the three bedrooms. The drawing room has comfortable green settees, and armchairs covered in fabric designed by Jean Munroe. A marble fireplace, fresh flowers, antique china, and plenty of magazines and books, gave me the feeling of being in somebody's tastefully furnished home, which indeed it is.

Peter and Jane Dunn, whose other Stone House is in Rushlake Green in East Sussex – conveniently close to Glyndebourne – have decided to provide in London the friendly country hospitality for which they have become well known. Bedrooms, decorated with Colefax & Fowler wallpapers are both elegant and homey (the hot-water bottle covers were designed by Nina Campbell). My room was upholstered in chintz patterned with crimson fuchsia and bordered with crimson. The television was hidden under the ruffles of a round corner table, and there was a comfortable easy-chair and a desk. Beside the bed – covered with well-ironed Egyptian cotton sheets – were a bowl of fruit and a jar of cookies.

There was a large wardrobe (with plenty of shelves) and there was even a good selection of books. The bathroom, white with marble surfaces and a green trim, was provided with a generous collection of toiletries and plenty of big white towels. The only meals provided at Stone House are breakfast and delicious light snacks. My breakfast, served on charming flower-bedecked Herend china, was a treat. As well as cereal, fruit compote, croissants, and rolls, there was yoghurt, honey from the Sussex Stone House bees, and home-made preserves.

Peter, a mostly-retired international businessman, and interior-decorator Jane will welcome you if they are present; currently they are helped by an ex-yuppie-City-stockbroker Oxford University theology graduate. Whichever Stone House you chose to visit, you will enjoy its decor, atmosphere, and food, and feel as welcome as you would when staying with relatives or close friends in a family home. Stone House is the ideal London hideaway.

The entrance hall (opposite, above), decorated in the manner of an 18th-century print room, is given a spacious appearance by the mirrored wall. A corner of the sitting room is shown above; one of the bedrooms appears opposite, below.

STONE HOUSE, Sydney Street, SW3. **Map reference** 5. **Tel**. Bookings: (0435) 830 553. **Telex** 957210 RLT G. **Owners** Peter and Jane Dunn. **Manager** Catherine Stevens. **Open** All year, except over Christmas. **Rooms** 3 double, all with bathroom (all with jacuzzi-style tub, 2 with shower), direct-dial phone, color TV, radio. **Facilities** Drawing room, luggage-only elevator, tours and transportation by Jaguar saloon arranged. **Restrictions** No dogs in public rooms. **Terms** Moderate. **Lunch/Dinner** Moderate (snacks only). **Credit cards** No; personal checks or cash only. **Nearest tube station** South Kensington, $\frac{1}{4}$ mile. **Hotel parking** No. NCP in Harrington Road, SW7, $\frac{1}{4}$ mile. **Local eating** (All in SW3) Walton's, 121 Walton Street; La Tante Claire, 68 Royal Hospital Road; San Frediano, 62 Fulham Road. **Local shopping** Chelsea boutiques; King's Road; Harrods and Knightsbridge stores. **Local interest** Hyde Park; Chelsea Hospital (flower show in May); Chelsea Physic Garden.

Step back in time

I found it to be, as David Copperfield said, "a wonderfully fine thing to walk about town with the key of my house in my pocket." This you can do if you stay at 43 Cloth Fair, in the heart of the City.

The Landmark Trust rescues historic houses, restores them, installs appropriate furniture and enough creature comforts to make them habitable all year round – heating, bathrooms, fully-equipped kitchens – and then allows people to enjoy the experience of living in them. The houses they rescue are all fascinating, and some are deliciously eccentric: a folly in the shape of a pineapple in Stirlingshire, a three-cornered Gothic temple in the landscaped gardens of Stowe, Buckinghamshire, a martello tower in Aldeburgh, Suffolk, and many more. I was delighted to find that the tiny 18th-century house they own in London is not only in one of the rare corners of the City to have survived both the Great Fire of 1666 and the World War II blitz, but was also once the property of John Betjeman, late great English eccentric and Poet Laureate.

This is not a hotel, and indeed you must bring your own bed-linen, and either cook for yourself, find a quick snack a few steps away, or seek out restaurant fare elsewhere. The caretaker next door runs a small jewelry store selling very attractive antique silver. He is extremely helpful and will advise on local geography. The Trust provides two books in each of its properties, one recording everything known of the history of the house and its surroundings, the other a log-book in which guests note their impressions. Both make absorbing reading.

Inside the front door is a minute hall for coats. Steep stairs lead up to a small cosy sitting room decorated with terracotta-colored oak-leaf patterned wallpaper and furnished with a round polished table and dining chairs, as well as olive-green easy chairs.

There are prints on the half-panelled walls, and the paintwork is white. Beside it is an immaculate small modern kitchen, with a small fridge, cooker, mixing bowls, pans, crockery, glasses, and cutlery – everything the two of you and two visitors would need. Above, there are twin beds with creamy-white woven covers and a spotless simple bathroom. Sitting room and bedroom both look out over the flower-filled churchyard of St Bartholomew the Great, built in 1123 and so one of the oldest churches in the city. Anyone who believes they already know London will find staying in Cloth Fair a new and magical experience.

43 Cloth Fair is the building on the left in the view from St Bartholomew's churchyard opposite, above. The bedroom appears opposite, below; above is a glimpse of the atmospheric interior of St Bartholomew's.

THE LANDMARK TRUST, 43 Cloth Fair, EC1. **Map reference** 17. **Bookings** Contact the owners, The Landmark Trust, Shottesbrooke, Maidenhead, Berkshire, SL6 3SW, tel. (062) 882 5925, sending a fee (currently £6), which brings you a complete book of all properties. **Open** All year. **Rooms** 1 twin, with bathroom (no shower). **Facilities** Sitting room, fully-equipped kitchen, door answerphone, caretaker Mon.–Fri. during business hours in next-door jewelry shop. (A second more simply-furnished house next door-but-one sleeps 4.) **Restrictions** None. **Terms** Moderate. **Lunch/Dinner** No. **Credit cards** All major cards. Payment to be made when booking, which should be well in advance of intended stay. **Nearest tube station** Barbican, 150 yds. **Parking** No. Nearest NCP in Smithfield, EC1. **Local eating/shopping** Many small restaurants, pubs, etc. nearby, and at St Katharine's Dock, which also has boutiques. Consult the caretaker. **Local interest** Within easy reach of the City, London's financial center, as well as St Paul's Cathedral, Wren's City churches, Smithfield Market, St Bartholomew the Great, St Bartholomew's Hospital, Guildhall, the Museum of London, Barbican Arts Center, Inns of Court.

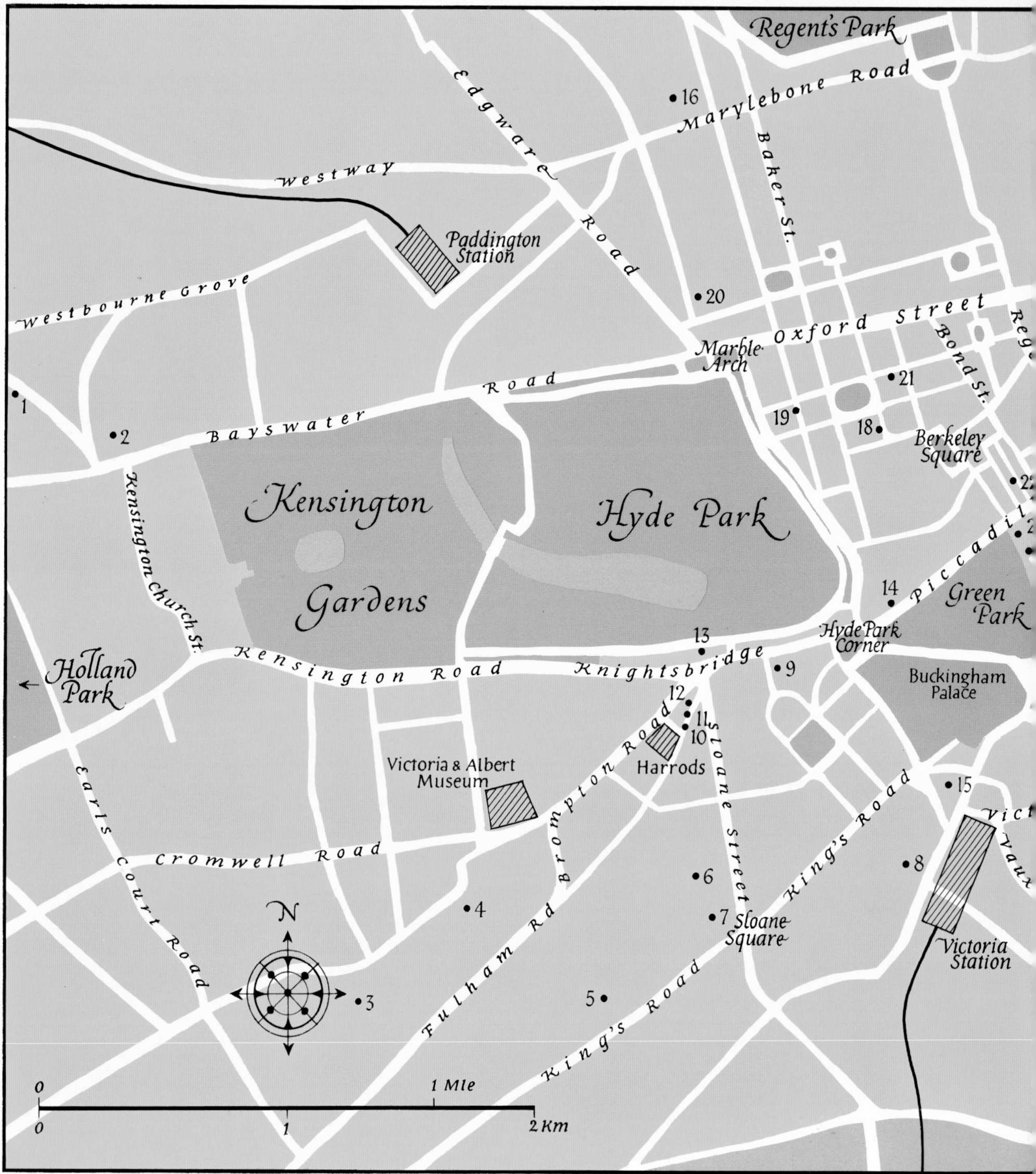

Map labels:

Regent's Park

Marylebone Road

Edgware Road

Westway

Paddington Station

Baker St.

•16

•20

Westbourne Grove

Marble Arch

Oxford Street

Bond St.

•21

19•

18•

Berkeley Square

Bayswater Road

•1

•2

Kensington Gardens

Hyde Park

Kensington Church St.

Holland Park

Kensington Road

Knightsbridge

Hyde Park Corner

•14 Piccadilly

Green Park

13•

•9

Buckingham Palace

12•

11•

10•

Victoria & Albert Museum

Harrods

Brompton Road

Sloane Street

Earls Court Road

Cromwell Road

Fulham Rd

•4

•6

•15

Vict... Vauxhall

•8

•7 Sloane Square

King's Road

Victoria Station

N

•3

5•

King's Road

0   1 Mle
0   1   2 Km

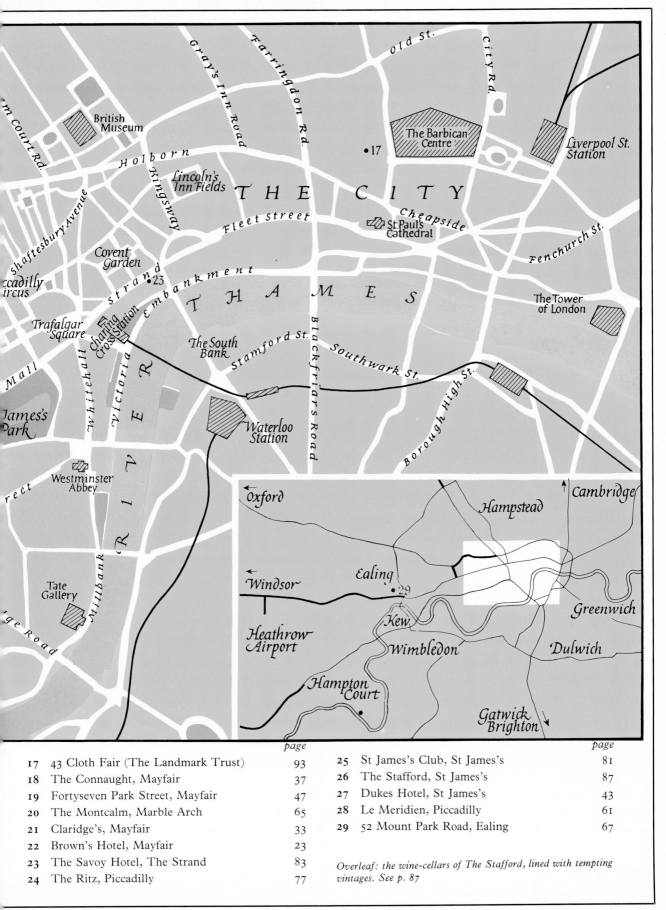

The map shows central London with labels including: m Court Rd, British Museum, Gray's Inn Road, Farringdon Rd, Old St., City Rd, The Barbican Centre, Liverpool St. Station, Holborn, Lincoln's Inn Fields, THE CITY, Kingsway, Shaftesbury Avenue, Fleet street, Cheapside, St Paul's Cathedral, Fenchurch St., Covent Garden, •23, Strand, Embankment, THAMES, The Tower of London, ccadilly ircus, Trafalgar Square, Charing Cross Station, Victoria, The South Bank, Stamford St., Blackfriars Road, Southwark St., Whitehall, Waterloo Station, Borough High St., ames's Park, Mall, RIVER, Westminster Abbey, Millbank, Tate Gallery, ge Road, •17.

Inset map: Oxford, Hampstead, Cambridge, Windsor, Ealing, •29, Kew, Greenwich, Heathrow Airport, Wimbledon, Dulwich, Hampton Court, Gatwick Brighton.

Overleaf: the wine-cellars of The Stafford, lined with tempting vintages. See p. 87